THE IDEA BOOK

by Fredrik Härén

INTERESTING BOOKS

Copyright © Fredrik Härén, Stockholm, Sweden.

Translated from Swedish by Fiona Miller

www.interesting.org

ISBN 91-975470-3-4

Design: André Wognum · www.wognum.se

The Idea Book was recently included in the American book
"The 100 Best Business Books of all Time" by Jack Covert
and Todd Sattersten.

That was a good idea —write it down!

This book is based on the premise that good ideas do not just appear by themselves: they need to be enticed out. Inspiration and motivation are two surefire ways of drawing out ideas. And it is just this that is the purpose of the book in your hand: to inspire and motivate you to come up with and write down lots of ideas.

This book contains more than 60 quick-to-read, inspiring sections about creativity as well as a host of relevant quotations by people like Albert Einstein and Ingvar Kamprad (founder of IKEA). Each section rounds off with an activity designed to help you tap your own well of creativity.

The book also contains 150 blank pages for your own ideas! When you have filled your book with notes, observations, doodles and ideas, then you will have a complete idea book.

Foreword

Thomas Edison understood the importance of writing down his ideas. He always had a notebook (or 'idea book') on him in which he wrote down his thoughts, ideas and observations. This jotting down of ideas was something he got from Leonardo Da Vinci, who produced a large number of sketches, notes and scribblings, often written in left-handed mirror-writing.

Edison may not have used backwards or reversed writing—but one thing is clear, he did write. He jotted down an idea as soon as it came to him. Whenever he was stuck or lacked inspiration, he went back to his notebooks to see if he could come up with any new ideas from the ones he had already written down. After Edison's death in 1931, an amazing 3,500 notebooks were found in his home.

This book hopes to follow in the footsteps of Edison and Da Vinci and motivate you to write down all your ideas. Make sure you do! Jot your idea down even if you think it is a mediocre one. Who knows? Sometime in the future you may develop a couple of roughly-written thoughts into a brilliant idea!

I hope that my creativity examples and activities will touch your imagination and entice out many ideas.

As Isabel Colgate said: *"It is not a bad idea to get in the habit of writing down one's thoughts. It saves one having to bother anyone else with them."* This is as good a reason as any other.

FREDRIK HÄRÉN

"Where all think alike, no one thinks very much."

WALTER LIPPMANN

Beep! Beep!

Dare to change branch — and find a hidden treasure of untapped ideas.

What would happen if Nokia or Sony Ericsson suddenly started producing cars? Well, you might be able to choose the ring signal — in other words, you could choose different horn melodies.

There is no doubt that car designers are innovative. They come up with many new ideas, like side airbags. However, the longer you work in a certain branch and the more expertise you have in your area, the harder it gets to look at your branch with new eyes. Quite simply, familiarity breeds contempt.

As far as the car designers at Ford are concerned, the car's horn is so taken for granted that they do not even question it. In the world of cars, the horn is always found on the wheel and when you press it, it goes beep. Even 21st century cars have a little picture of an 18th century bugle to signify the horn's function.

ACTIVITY

Bring in outside experts to solve a problem, or use your own expertise to develop a branch that you have no experience of. Best of all: take a couple of people from different branches and see what solution they come up with together.

By the way, what would a mobile phone developed by Ford's designers be like?

"Creativity can solve almost any problem. The creative act, the defeat of habit by originality, overcomes everything."
GEORGE LOIS

The world's first creativity test

Bring out more ideas.

BACKGROUND

Many regard J.P. Guilford as the father of modern creativity. At a psychology conference nearly 50 years ago, he held an attention-grabbing speech about creativity that sparked off a great interest in it. An interest that grows larger every year.

Guilford's own story is an interesting one. He was a psychologist who, during the Second World War, worked on personality tests designed to pick out the most suitable bomber pilot candidates. In order to do this, Guilford used intelligence tests, a grading system and personal interviews. He was annoyed because the Air Force had also assigned a retired air force pilot without psychological training to help in the selection process. Guilford did not have much faith in the retired officer's experience.

It turned out that Guilford and the retired officer chose different candidates. After a while, their work was evaluated and, surprisingly, the pilots chosen by Guilford were shot down and killed much more frequently than those selected by the retired pilot. Guilford later confessed to being so depressed about sending so many pilots to their deaths that he considered suicide. Instead of this course of action, he decided to find out why the pilots chosen by the retired pilot had fared so much better than those he had selected.

The old pilot said that he had asked one question to all the would-be pilots: *"What would you do if your plane was shot at by German anti-aircraft when you were flying over Germany?"* He ruled out everyone who answered, *"I'd fly higher"*. Those who answered, *"I don't know—maybe I'd dive"* or *"I'd zigzag"* or *"I'd roll and try to avoid the gunfire by turning"* all gave the wrong answer according to the rule book. The retired pilot, however, chose his candidates from the group that answered incorrectly. The soldiers who followed the manual were also very predictable and that is where Guilford failed. All those he chose answered according to the manual. The problem was that even the Germans knew that you should fly higher when under fire and their fighter planes therefore lay in wait above the clouds, ready to shoot down the American pilots. In other words, it was the creative pilots who survived more often than those who may have been more intelligent, but who stuck by the rules!

Guilford suddenly realized that it was a talent to be able to think differently, unexpectedly, creatively, and so he decided to study this skill further. It was his aim to find a way of selecting the most suitable pilots by identifying those creative candidates who improvised and came up with unexpected solutions.

One of Guilford's first creativity tests for the Air Force was asking candidates to find as many uses for a brick as possible. Although simple, this is a good way of testing someone's creativity. Some just churn out an endless number of uses faster than you can write them down while others think for minutes before coming up with five uses.

This is also a good way of kick starting the creativity skills of a person or group.

ACTIVITY

You guessed it! This activity is, of course: How many uses for a brick can you think of? Start by trying to come up with 50 different uses in 15 minutes.

Of course, thinking of new uses for a brick does not raise efficiency in a company or lead to innovative products, but it is an interesting test to find out who is not held back by what they have learnt.

Metaphors are strong mountains

Realize the value of identifying a metaphor.

We think in metaphors—and we do it more often than we realize. A metaphor is an excellent way of explaining something new by using a toolbox of old experiences.

Have you ever realized that we often use metaphors taken from the world of birds to describe ideas? We brood over a thought, hatch ideas that are as delicate as eggshells and when an idea really takes off, it soars away on the wings of creativity. The whole idea process is similar to that of a bird's development.

Another classic example arose when a group of arms manufacturers were developing a new weapon for the air force. They could not come up with any ideas, so a member of the group suggested that they change metaphor. *"Imagine that we're in the desert,"* he said to the others. *"Describe what you see." "I see a cactus,"* said one. *"I see an oasis,"* said another. *"I see a sidewinder,"* said a third. A sidewinder is a snake that can hone in on its prey by detecting its body heat. Suddenly, one of the engineers had a brainwave. *"Couldn't we make a missile capable of detecting the heat from an enemy engine?"* They worked on this idea and developed the highly successful heat-seeking missile, the Sidewinder.

Which metaphor best describes your branch? Which metaphor have you chosen for the problem you are working on now? It is often the case that we have not identified the metaphor that is relevant for us. And by not identifying it, we cannot see if the metaphor has forced us into a corner or not.

ACTIVITY

How can we generate ideas by developing a metaphor? Can we create a nest of ideas? Can we feed newly-hatched thoughts? Must an idea cry out for food? Do migratory ideas develop best by flying south when winter comes? Try to develop the idea/egg/bird metaphor.

Always try to identify and develop the metaphor that forms the basis of the idea you are currently working on.

"An invasion of armies can be resisted, but not an idea whose time has come." VICTOR HUGO

Edison's idea quota

*Understand the importance of coming up with a multitude of ideas
as opposed to a handful.*

BACKGROUND

Thomas Alva Edison was a man who realized that you had to come up
with many ideas in order to have one good one. Edison was, undoubtedly,
an inventive genius. He held the world record for the greatest number
of inventions. He invented the gramophone and the incandescent light
bulb, developed a storage battery and improved film projectors as well as
founding what is today the world's largest company, General Electric.

Edison realized, however, that good ideas do not come about by themselves, so he enforced an idea quota on himself and his employees. His
own quota was this: A minor invention every ten days, and a major invention every six months.

ACTIVITY

Force yourself to come up with more ideas! When facing a problem,
think of 50 different solutions. Many of the ideas will not be good ones,
but the chances are that the first ideas will not be the best ones anyway.
Practise finding many solutions to many problems. Make a habit of asking
yourself, *"What other ways are there of solving this problem?"* Do not give up
until you have thought of at least three new solutions. Remember that
there are always different ways of solving a problem.

"To improve is to change; to be perfect is to change often." WINSTON CHURCHILL

The unhappy professor

Challenge the impossible.

BACKGROUND

There is a story about a grumpy university professor who was always bitter and angry. In fact, he was so grumpy that many postgraduates were afraid of him. Finally, one student gathered enough courage to ask the professor why he was always so grumpy. *"Well, you see,"* said the professor, *"back in the sixties when I was as young as you, we came up with the ideas for everything that is now a reality: the mobile phone, the automatic lawnmower, computer networks and so on. And now, when all this is possible, I retire in a year."*

The poor professor was bitter because he had not been young in an age where the electronic circuit was small enough and cheap enough to be fitted into anything and everything. He was annoyed because it was no longer technology that stood in the way of what could be developed, but the human imagination.

Learn to question the statement that things are impossible to do. Today's rapid development means that it is now possible to accomplish many things that were previously considered impossible. At the same time, we must also learn to set ourselves new impossibilities: otherwise, our thoughts run the risk of stagnating. As we solve yesterday's impossibilities, so must we find new impossibilities to solve tomorrow.

ACTIVITY

Describe something in your organization that is currently impossible, but which will soon become possible to achieve. Describe the effect it will have when the impossible becomes possible. How can you benefit from these changes?

"Any business arrangement that is not profitable to the other person will in the end prove unprofitable for you. The bargain that yields mutual satisfaction is the only one that is apt to be repeated." B. C. FORBES

"A thing is not right
because we do it.

A method is not good
because we use it.

Equipment is not the
best because we own it."

JOHN ALDAIR

'Broken' monitors

The importance of asking the right question.

BACKGROUND

We often learn how to find the answer to something, but seldom how to find the question. Learning how to ask questions is something we could all do with improving. Just questioning your own organization to see if you can find a better way of running it, is the first step in the right direction. Know how to ask the right question and you are already halfway there.

One of the cafés in an international European airport was often full. The problem was that people sat nursing their coffees for a long time as they waited for their planes to depart. The café asked itself: *How can we encourage our customers to vacate the tables more quickly?* Their first ideas were probably along the lines of uncomfortable chairs, a seat charge, clear the tables immediately and so forth. However, the idea they finally decided upon was this: to turn off the flight monitors in the café! This made people worry about missing their flights, which led to them looking for monitors that worked, thus leaving empty tables. When the café had enough empty tables, the flight monitors suddenly started working again to attract new customers.

Formulating a question in different ways can help you look at a problem from different angles. In the case above, for example, you can find new angles by putting the question in another way: *How can we sell more?* So, instead of finding solutions to the problem of getting people to vacate the tables more quickly, you can also come up with solutions such as set up a take-away stand so that people can have a snack or drink by the departure gates, or sell picnic bags that passengers can take onto the planes with them and so on.

ACTIVITY

Ask more questions and learn to question things that work well in order to see if they can work even better!

When facing a problem, formulate it as a question and then try to find several answers. If you get stuck, ask the question in another way. You can always formulate a problem in many different ways.

"When you are a Bear of Very Little Brain, and you Think of Things, you find sometimes that a Thing which seemed very Thingish inside you is quite different when it gets out into the open and has other people looking at it."
WINNIE THE POOH

About squeazle and other words

Find the courage to invent new words in order to invent new ideas.

BACKGROUND

"Can you believe it?" said Pippi dreamily. "Can you believe it was me that thought of it? Me, of all people, that made it up?"

"What is it you've made up?" asked Tommy and Annika both together. It did not surprise them in the least that Pippi hade made something up— she was always doing it—but they wanted to know what it was. *"But what is it, Pippi?"*

"A new word," said Pippi, looking at Tommy and Annika as if she had only just caught sight of them, "a brand new word."

"What word?" asked Tommy.

"A really super word," said Pippi, "one of the superest I've ever heard."

"Tell us!" said Annika.

"Squeazle," said Pippi triumphantly.

"Squeazle?" repeated Tommy. "What does it mean?"

"I only wish I knew," said Pippi. "All I know is that it doesn't mean a vacuum cleaner."

This text comes from the book Pippi in the South Seas by Astrid Lindgren.

Describing a new idea with old words can sometimes ruin the effect of the idea. Don't be afraid to find new words that describe your idea better. Wheel, radio, TV and Internet—yes, all new words arise in order to explain a new phenomenon that did not exist earlier. So, don't be scared of coming up with your own 'squeazle' word!

Using old words to describe new phenomena to their full extent is as unlikely to succeed as using old seeds to grow new fruit. Indeed, using old words for new ideas often impedes development. In the early 1990s, many people described the Internet as 'a brochure on the Net', which led to the Internet efforts of many companies becoming no more than online brochures. Before broadband was called broadband, it was known as Video on Demand (VOD). This, in turn, meant that many broadband demos only showed how you could download films via broadband. If mobile phones were called PDAs (Personal Digital Assistants), then I am convinced that the acceptance of mobile data services would be much higher than it is today.

ACTIVITY

Come up with a new word to describe your project, problem or your suggested solution to a problem. The word can be a combination of two existing words (e.g. infotainment) or it can be a completely new word. Use the new word as your starting point and see if it can create new ideas.

Bird — Fish — or Fird?

Create new ideas by combining old ones.

BACKGROUND

By definition, an idea is one or more old ideas combined to form something new. There are very few ideas that are not, in fact, a combination of earlier ideas. Can you even think of an idea that is not a mixture of at least two earlier ones?

You can create a whole new idea by taking two established ones and putting them together. Just look at the newspaper *Metro* that took the concept of the free newspaper and the morning paper to come up with the free morning paper.

Another clear example of this is ICQ. It is neither an e-mail program, nor a chat program. It is 50% e-mail and 50% chat. By being a combination of both and neither-nor, the creators cornered a highly desirable niche that is unique in fulfilling a pent-up need. In just a few years, ICQ had 20 million users because it did not compete with existing products but created a completely new one.

ACTIVITY

Take two ideas and put them together to see what happens. This often creates a more interesting idea than the two orginal ideas individually. Then combine three different ideas. Or four. Or two new ones...

"High technology obeys the iron law of revolution, the more you change, the more you have to change, you have to be willing to accept the fact that in this game the rules keep changing." BILL JOY

Looking for needles in a haystack

Look for many different answers.

BACKGROUND

Albert Einstein was once asked, *"What's the difference between you and the rest of us?"* He replied, *"If you are asked to look for a needle in a haystack, then you search until you find it, whereas I search until I find all the needles."*

Then there is the story about how Einstein gave his students a test. They looked at the test and said in surprise, *"Professor, this is the same test as the one you gave us last time!"*

"Yes," he replied. *"The questions are the same, but the answers are different."*

Both these stories show how Einstein always looked for several different answers. And, of course, he was right: there are always many different, right ways of doing something.

ACTIVITY

When someone finds a solution to a problem, ask the question: *Can't we do this in another way?* People will criticize you and think that you are being awkward if you do not give in when someone has a good idea. But stand your ground: there probably is an even better idea out there just waiting to be found!

If you do get criticism, then you can always quote the Swedish Minister of Trade and Industry, Leif Pagrotsky: *"People stand in line with different errands that they expect me to decide upon and take responsibility for. So, when I persist in asking for the opposite to happen instead, I often create a lot of extra work. But I do it anyway as I believe it is important."*

"The only constant in our business is that everything is changing. We have to take advantage of change and not let it take advantage of us. We have to be ahead of the game." MICHAEL DELL

"A question that sometimes drives me hazy: am I or are the others crazy?"

ALBERT EINSTEIN

Curiosity fed the cat

See metaphors as creativity tools.

Metaphors are excellent tools for developing and clarifying ideas. However, metaphors and proverbs are also excellent tools for questioning ingrained opinions.

The saying *Curiosity killed the cat* is often used to discourage the eagerness of creative and curious people to break new ground. OK—some poor cat probably has been run over because it was too curious. However, if we re-write the expression so that it says *curiosity fed the cat*, then we have suddenly turned it into something positive, in which the the cat survives thanks to its creativity and curiosity. By twisting and turning metaphors and proverbs, we can find new ways of illuminating 'truths' that, in turn, make it easier to find new solutions.

Just because you can come up with a saying about something does not mean it is true. Take time, for example. We say, *"Time flies when you're having fun!"*—which is evidence that time passes quickly when something is fun. We also say, *"It was such a moving moment that time stood still."*—which is evidence that time does not pass at all. So, which expression is telling the truth about time? Both! A metaphor or expression can be used to prove whatever you like, which just goes to prove that it does not prove anything!

Many people believe that the proverb *"The grass is greener on the other side"* is true. But if we just change it a little to *"The grass is greener on your own side"*, then it has suddenly become a positive force, instead of a negative one. All it takes are two little words to change the entire meaning of the proverb!

Proverbs and sayings have a stronger influence on the way we view the world than most of us realize. It is only when we dare challenge these truths that we can find new ways to new thoughts.

Remember that sayings have a surprisingly powerful way of changing opinions into truths. Just as with statistics, you can 'prove' anything with a proverb or a saying.

Which metaphor is your line of business based upon? Can you re-write this metaphor to change its meaning, and by doing so, can you use this new metaphor to develop your business?

"The grass is greener on your own side."

PROVERB

The curious creature of habit

Break old ways of thinking.

We humans are curious creatures of habit. If we were not curious about the world, then we would still be living in caves. However, at the same time we are confirmed creatures of habit. As soon as we have learnt something, we keep on doing it in the same old way. And it is just as well: for if we were continually to question everything, then we would probably go mad. The problem is, however, that our brains trick us into thinking along the same old lines a bit too successfully!

It is, after all, natural for us to imitate. Most animals imitate their parents, thus learning how to fly, hunt, swim and so on. In the same way, children listen to their parents and learn a language. It is natural to imitate. To learn and then do the direct opposite is unnatural.

An idea is similar to the transformation of information. Give 100 people access to the same information and 99 of them will consider it to be a fact. One person out of 100 will think: *"Mm, but what if we could..."* Just as in nature, 99% of these information exchanges are not so successful, while the hundredth one makes sure that development goes forward.

There is a story about an advertising executive in Los Angeles who was so fed up of being stuck in a rut that he forced himself to find new ways of getting to work every day. He never took the same route to work in his nine years of commuting. (Towards the end, he was forced to reverse down one-way streets in order not to repeat himself.)

ACTIVITY

Identify something at work that you always do in the same old way. Next time you come to do that task, ask yourself if you can do it in another way instead. Consider it a creative challenge to find 20 ways of doing that routine task and do not give in until you have succeeded.

The idea is not necessarily to find a new solution to everyday tasks, but to help you identify all the things in life that we do out of pure habit.

"Philosophers have only interpreted the world. The point however is to change it." KARL MARX

Fragile ideas

Realize how vulnerable ideas are.

BACKGROUND

Advertising boss, Charles Browe, aptly described just how delicate an idea is before it finds footing and becomes established when he said, *"An idea is fragile. It can be killed by a scornful smile or a yawn. It can be mowed down by irony and scared to death by a cold look."*

Howard Gardner stated cynically, *"Most cultures throughout human history have not liked creative individuals. They ignore them or they kill them. It is a very effective way of stopping creativity."*

Throughout Europe, we have had the unfortunate tendency to burn innovative and creative women at the stake on the excuse that they must be witches in cahoots with the devil. It is easy to see that, because of the risk of being burnt at the stake all those years ago, many creative people must have hidden their radical ideas instead of testing them. And it was understandable, of course.

Even today it is often difficult for new ideas to be accepted. Half the work of being creative is daring to go forward with your ideas, even if you are almost certain of meeting resistance at the beginning.

ACTIVITY

Next time you present an idea and it gets shot down—for goodness sake, do not let yourself become down-hearted! Instead, decide to fight for your idea, no matter what people think. What is the worst that can happen? That you are burnt at the stake? Hardly!

"Managing and innovation did not always fit comfortably together. That's not surprising. Managers are people who like order. They like forecasts to come out as planned. In fact managers are often judged on how much order they produce. Innovation, on the other hand, is often a disorderly process. Many times, perhaps most times, innovation does not turn out as planned. As a result, there is tension between managers and innovation." LEWIS L. LEHRO ABOUT THE FIRST YEARS AT 3M.

"These days innovation is the corporate mantra. The problem is that the majority of companies doesn't practice their mantra. They still focus on short time profit since that can be measured and innovation can't." ALEXANDER LOUDON

"I can't understand why people are frightened of new ideas. I'm frightened of the old ones."

JOHN CAGE

The 1968 Olympics, Mexico

Learn to ignore what you have learnt.

BACKGROUND

Albert Einstein exclaimed wisely, *"Imagination is more important than knowledge!"* But what is the difference between knowledge and creativity? Let's take a brief look into the fantastic world of sports to see if we can find some illuminating examples.

The whole point of the high jump is to jump over a horizontal bar. The person who jumps highest is the winner. Up until 1968, there were two ways of jumping over the bar. You could either dive over (hands first, then head followed by the rest of the body, face downwards) or you could hurdle over (like a hurdler, one leg going over first, then the other). This was how to do the high jump, and the collected wisdom of the day was all about the best way of diving or hurdling over the bar. If you wanted to be a top high jumper, then you could find out everything there was to know about these two methods.

Of course, knowing everything about the high jump does not guarantee that you will be a good high jumper, but the odds are undoubtedly better. However, one day, Fosbury came along. He was a high jumper studying medicine, who had begun to think for himself. Fosbury began to consider how the human body was actually constructed and he suddenly realized that the smartest way of jumping over a high bar was probably not by diving or hurdling, but by jumping over with his back to the bar.

He developed his new technique and dazzled everyone at the 1968 Olympics in Mexico by taking the gold. Looking for a new way of doing the high jump was more valuable than just accepting the existing knowledge on the subject.

If we can find a new way of doing a banal thing like the high jump, then we must realize that there are probably many more complicated things we can do in completely new ways. Not all the new methods we come up with will be good ones, some may even be forbidden, but others will be very good ideas. And in order to find the brilliant ideas, we must dare to ignore what we already know.

Another sports example about how valuable it can be not to do what everyone says you should do, comes from Sweden. Jan Boklöv ignored everything people said about ski-jumping. Instead of jumping with straight skis, he held them out at an angle. The judges' first reaction was to deduct points for jumping in an ugly fashion. However, they soon changed their minds and, today, everyone jumps like Boklöv without thinking it is ugly!

ACTIVITY

How would you design a course to teach people to ignore existing knowledge?

Imagination is more important than knowledge.

ALBERT EINSTEIN

Find the bug

Identify what irritates you.

BACKGROUND

Linus Torvalds, the inventor of Linux, says the following in his book: *Just for Fun.* "*What got me interested in operating systems: I bought a floppy controller so I wouldn't have to use the microdrives, but the driver that came with the floppy controller was bad so I ended up writing my own. In the process of writing that I found some bugs in the operating system—or at least a discrepancy between what the documentation said the operating system would do and what it actually did. I found it because something I had written didn't work.*

My code is always, um, perfect. So I knew it had to be something else, and I went in and disassembled the operating system."

This is how the Linux operating system was born. A success story that just goes to prove that it is a good idea to search for solutions to things that bug you.

This is harder than you imagine, however. We humans have a tendency to think that the status quo is relatively good. At the same time, we get annoyed about things because we believe that that is how they must be, instead of identifying what bugs us and finding a solution.Only a few years ago, we were all annoyed because the banks shut at three. Now we are irritated because we have to enter a long security code when we stay up late on a Thursday night to pay our bills over the Internet. When the banks succeed in solving this problem, what else will we find to get angry about?

Wherever there is a group of disgruntled people, there is a market for a new product or service. Unfortunately, however, we are all too seldom aware of the fact that we have a problem. On the arrival of the answering machine, many of us wondered how we had managed before. Then number presentation came along and we, once again, wondered how we had managed without it. The advent of the mobile phone made us wonder how we had survived with only a land line. As soon as we began to send SMS messages, we realized that it solved a problem we did not know we had—and so on.

With hindsight, it is easy to see that many of these services could have been launched years earlier if we had only realized how much less frustrated we would feel. Which pent-up irritation will we solve next?

ACTIVITY

Write down ten things that bug you. Write down the ten most common complaints about your product or service. Try to come up with an improvement that not only solves your irritating problem, but which also makes your service that little bit better.

"One should never impose one's views on a problem;
one should rather study it, and in time a solution will reveal itself." ALBERT EINSTEIN

73

Find other perspectives

Understand the value of diversity.

BACKGROUND

Soki Choi is the founder of the company, Blue Factory. Soki's parents come from Korea, but moved to Sweden where Soki herself was born and raised. Soki says that the greatest advantage of her multi-cultural upbringing is not the fact that it is easier to understand different cultures, but that she realizes that the truth is not absolute.

When Soki was growing up, it was natural to celebrate both the Chinese New Year as well as the Swedish one. By growing up in a bi-cultural home, Soki learnt always to see things from two different perspectives. When you realize that there are always two (or more) ways of looking at things, then you quickly realize that there can never be only one absolute truth.

ACTIVITY

Most companies are very bad at using the potential that can be found in people with diverse cultural backgrounds. How can we help companies become better at this?

"Every fool can see what is wrong. See what is good in it!" WINSTON CHURCHILL

Stuck in a metaphor—again

Question metaphors.

Back in the 1800s, the locomotive industry was the most innovative branch that could be imagined. When looking back at these trains today, it is hard to understand what was so innovative about the industry then.

When the first trains were produced, doctors warned against building railways out in the countryside as farmers would go mad when they saw such modern technology! When the train was invented, it was regarded as a horse and cart on rails. (The engine, for example, was called the iron horse.)

This meant that those working on this revolutionary invention (for its time), found it difficult to think outside the metaphor with which they chose to compare their invention. For example, it took years before train compartments were designed with aisles in the middle so that passengers could go from compartment to compartment. Until then, trains were no more than a number of compartments that sat one behind the other: in other words, they were built just like carts on rails.

Now, maybe it did not matter much if you could not move between compartments, even if it was more practical. However, the fact remains that this inability to think beyond established experience meant that lives were wasted. The comparison of the train to the horse and cart meant that passengers sat on, rather than in, the compartments. This is what you did in the time of the horse and cart—so this is what you did now, even though it made no sense to have passengers sitting on the roof.

As a result, 72 (!) people died from falling off trains in as late as 1866, according to the book, Cracking Creativity. Not thinking outside the box cost these poor people their lives.

ACTIVITY

Which simplified metaphor does your company/product use and how long will it take before you can let go of the old metaphor and move on to something new?

The white man

See the obvious from other points of view.

In the book *The White Man*, you can read about the South Pacific chief, Tuiavii, from the Samoan island of Upolu and his journey around Europe at the beginning of the 1900s. On his return home, he wrote down his thoughts about everything that he had seen and experienced in the land of the white man, whom he called Papalagi.

Tuiavii found it difficult to understand why the Western way of living was deemed to be so civilized and advanced. As he saw our way of life from another perspective, he managed to formulate many clear-sighted thoughts about phenomena that we take for granted. Here are some examples:

He described a newspaper as many pieces of paper that everyone reads in the morning so that everyone knows what they should think, and so that everyone thinks the same.

He described work like this: *"Having a profession means doing the same thing all the time and so often that you get tired of it."*

By looking at a culture from a distance, you can see the problems and possibilities that those who live in that culture cannot see.

ACTIVITY

Ask yourself this: How would the South Pacific chief, Tuiavii, have described your organization?

"In the modern world of business, it is useless to be a creative original thinker unless you can also sell what you create. Management cannot be expected to recognize a good idea unless it is presented to them by a good salesman."
DAVID M. OGILVY

"The prediction I can make with the highest confidence is that the most amazing discoveries will be the ones we are not today wise enough to foresee."

CARL SAGAN

Baby food for prisoners

See the importance of doing the opposite once in a while.

BACKGROUND

There was a chief of police in Florida who had a lot of problems every spring as this was when hordes of college students descended on his city to celebrate the spring break. The problem for both city and chief of police was that some of the students celebrated a little too much! For many young Americans, the spring break is a time to drink and smoke and do as many crazy things as possible in as short a time as possible.

The poor chief of police and his officers had their hands full taking care of the young students who had drunk too much or committed a petty crime. The police put the young men in drunk cells, but this did not alleviate the problem. Quite the opposite, in fact, as it was a cool and macho thing to have spent the night in a cell. The men bragged to their friends about having been in prison. The police tried stricter punishments: the college students were left in lock-up for two days instead of one; they got only bread and water; they got only water. Nothing worked. The chief of police realized then that there was no point in continuing to make the punishment more severe as it had no effect.

In the USA, it is quite common for people to use the 'carry on banging your head against a brick wall if it does not work' method. You can, for example, get a 1,000 year sentence—as if this were more frightening than a sentence of 500 years! This chief of police, however, was not a typical American chief of police and he thought the opposite. So, instead of treating the college students more and more like men, he began to treat them like children. He locked them up for only one night, but gave them baby food. It is not much fun to come out of your cell when your friends know that you have eaten baby food. Suddenly, it was no longer so manly to have been in prison.

ACTIVITY

When you feel that you cannot solve a problem, then try doing the opposite. When all the airlines concentrated on improving their services, along came Ryanair and took away the frills—and instead offered passengers very cheap flights. Today, Ryanair is one of Europe's most successful airline companies.

"Many ideas grow better when transplanted into another mind than in the one where they sprang up."
OLIVER WENDELL HOLMES JR.

"How I was able to discover the law of gravity? By thinking of it continuously."

ISAAC NEWTON

Mix the umixable

See the context where there is not one.

Leonardo Da Vinci once wrote that he tried to mix the umixable. And, indeed, finding a pattern where you least expect one is an art. You can find connections everywhere, if you only dare open yourself up to them.

The guy who invented the smoke alarm is said to have been watching the Phantom of the Opera in a theatre when he noticed how the actors nearly disappeared in the smoke that was used to create fog in the musical. It dawned on him that a smoke machine would provide excellent protection against burglars if it could only pump out enough smoke to fill a whole room. Going from theatre visit to burglar alarm may seem an unlikely route, but by being open to new impressions, you can find answers in the most unexpected places.

When Morse was working on making morse signals strong enough to transmit from coast to coast in the USA, he observed a change of horses and realized that he could boost the signals by establishing exchange stations at regular intervals.

ACTIVITY

When trying to solve a problem, try to find a connection to something that seems to have nothing at all in common with the problem. For example, how can an egg be used to improve telephony? What does a sewing machine have to do with broadband? This kind of activity is an excellent creativity booster as our brains actually thrive on finding connections between different things, no matter how unrelated. Don't be put off if your first ideas seem unrealistic and crazy. Think and reflect; accept the wild ideas that pop up and try to turn them into sensible, business-like solutions.

"There is a natural opposition among men to anything they haven't thought of themselves." BARNES WALLES

The creativity process

A quick overview of the different stages in a creative process.

There are many theories about creativity and many models to show how the creative process works. I am not going to describe these processes in detail because of the following two reasons:

1) Most of the descriptions of the creative process are more or less the same. Okay—the process may be divided into three, four or five stages, and they may be called different names—but they all describe a similar process.

2) No one becomes more creative by trying to follow the different stages of the creative process. To put it quite simply, I believe that those who try to become more creative by following a description of the creative process are on the wrong track. You do not become more creative by studying the details of the creative process, just as you do not become a top chef by reading a list of ingredients or recipes. You become a top chef by cooking and by training your culinary skills; likewise you become more innovative by training yourself to come up with ideas.

I cannot think of a worse way of trying to be more creative than by reading through a checklist. For those of you still interested in a description of the creative process, then I recommend you read James Webb Young, Helmholtz, M. F. Rubinstein or Jack Foster. They all describe the different stages in a similar way:

1) Collect information.

2) Organize your material.

3) Let your subconscious absorb the information.

4) Come up with an idea.

5) Evaluate or carry out the idea.

ACTIVITY

If you want to become richer in ideas, then throw out your checklists and force yourself to take part in more creative activities like learning how to paint, writing a poem, solving more problems and constantly forcing yourself to find several solutions to your problem as well as asking yourself how you could do the opposite. Or, as the author of *Uncommon Genius* writes: *"Staying loose, allowing yourself the freedom to ramble, opening yourself up to the outside influences, keeping a flexible mind willing to entertain all sorts of notions and avenues—this is the attitude that is most appropriate for the start of any project where the aim is to generate something new."* Amen.

"One should recognize and manage innovation as it really is; a tumultuous, somewhat random, interactive learning process linking a worldwide network of knowledge sources to the subtle unpredictability of customers' end uses."
JAMES BRIAN QUINN

The barometer and the house

How many ways are there of measuring the height of a house?

BACKGROUND

A teacher once set this as a test question: How can you measure the height of a house with a barometer? The teacher wanted the students to say that you measure the air pressure on the ground and then the air pressure at the top of the house. Then, by using a formula, you can work out the height. One student, however, thought that this was too simple, so he suggested the following: *"If I were to measure the height of a house, I would climb up onto the roof and lower the barometer tied to a piece of string until it reached the ground. I would then measure the length of the string."* The teacher marked this answer as wrong.

But our friend, the obstinate student, was not wrong. After all, he succeeded in measuring the height of the house with a barometer. The student did not give in; he asked the teacher to give him another chance to answer the question.

This time, he wrote: *"If I were to measure the height of a house, I would climb up onto the roof and drop the barometer from there. I would time the process to see how long it takes for the barometer to reach the ground. From this, I could calculate the height of the house."*

Once again, the teacher gave him zero. This time, the student suggested: *"I would climb up the stairs in the house, and on the way up, I would take measurements against the wall. On reaching the top, I would multiply the number of times I used the barometer by its length and then I could work out how tall the house is."* The student was told off again.

"Maybe the teacher is expecting a more mathematical answer," he thought. His next idea was this: *"I would place the barometer next to the house and measure its shadow. Then, I would measure the height of the barometer and the house's shadow in order to work out how the height of the house."* The teacher did not like this answer either!

By now, the student was so fed up that he wrote: *"I would go to the house, knock on the door and say to the occupant, 'If you don't tell me how tall your house is, I'll beat you to death with my barometer!'"*

According to an e-mail circulating round the Internet, the student in question was Nils Bohr, a Danish Nobel prize winner. As another Nobel prize winner, Linus Pauling, once said: *"The best way to get a good idea is to have lots of ideas."* And, of course, it is just this ability to look for several answers to a question that many Nobel prize winners have in common.

ACTIVITY

Our search for the 'right' answer is not something we learn to do only in school. Unfortunately, we also carry this attitude over to our working lives. Next time you have a problem to solve at work, ask yourself if you can find a solution in another way. And don't give up until you have thought of at least seven completely different ways of solving the problem.

If you don't tell me how tall your house is, I'll beat you to death with my barometer...

A taxi driver who does not know the way

The benefit of taking away basic requirements.

BACKGROUND

A good way of coming up with new ideas is to write down the basic requirements set by an organization and then take away one of them.

Imagine that we want to improve the taxi business in a big city like New
York or London. The two basic requirements for a taxi driver are that 1)
he can find the way and 2) he can drive. Let us now take away the first
requirement—that he can find the way. Many large cities suffer from a
shortage of taxi drivers, which in turn leads to long queues and annoyed
customers. These cities usually have a large number of unemployed people who could easily drive a taxi, but do not have a taxi licence. In order
to get a licence, you have to be able to find your way around all the areas
in the city. Many of the unemployed are not sure if they could pass this
part of the taxi test, and so do not even attempt to get a licence.

Now imagine that there is such a thing as the *?-taxi*. A question mark
taxi is like a normal taxi, except that it is driven by a trainee who has not
yet got a taxi licence. You cannot, of course, pre-order such a taxi (as he
would not be able to find his way to pick you up), but you can flag them
down on the street. After all, nine out of ten times you know how to get
to where you are going when you get into a taxi. On these occasions, you
could use a question mark taxi. Sure—you have to give the driver direc-
tions, but as thanks for your help, you only pay 80% of the normal fare.

The advantages of question mark taxis are numerous:

More taxis on the streets.

Full fare taxis can take care of more bookings.

*The drivers of question mark taxis earn money while learning to find their
way around the city.*

*When they know the city inside and out, they can take their test and work
as full fare taxi drivers.*

This example just goes to prove that you can have a good idea by taking away one of the basic requirements.

ACTIVITY

Can you come up with any good ideas when the second requirement is taken away? Just imagine a taxi driver who cannot drive...

Which basic requirements does your branch or organization have? Write them down and then take away one of the requirements and see what ideas this gives rise to!

Think again

Entice out more ideas.

Albert Einstein once said, *"I think and think for months and years. Ninety-nine times, the conclusion is false. The hundredth time I am right."* Most ideas that see the light of day are just that: ideas. They are killed at once and never tried out. And that is just as well, as many ideas are not worth carrying out. Many ideas that are carried out fail for different reasons—and every time you come up with a new idea, you certainly hear all about these failures! There was, for example, a lot of malicious pleasure in the failure of London's Millennium Dome and Jonas Birgersson's IT company, Framfab.

However, if you want to get anywhere, then you have to dare to try new things. To succeed, you have to dare to fail. Indeed, maybe it helps to be a little crazy if you want your new ideas to succeed. Maybe you have to be brave enough to fail in order to succeed in doing something new. (Just look at Columbus, for example.)

Edison carried out 9,000 experiments before producing the most suitable light bulb, and 50,000 before inventing the storage battery. He did not see himself as failing thousands of times, however—but rather as if he had learnt thousands of ways in which the experiment did not work. His view was that he developed his inventions in a large number of stages. Every failure was but a step closer to a working innovation.

ACTIVITY

It may seem depressing to come up with masses of ideas that are too bad to use, but if you want to come up with that one really good idea, then you have to have the courage to think of lots of bad ideas, too. It is like exercising: it is the last ab crunches or push-ups that really count. When you think that you have thought of enough ideas, then sit back down and come up with ten more.

"It's ironic that companies pay CEO's millions upon millions to unlock shareholder wealth, but seem incapable of funnelling six and seven figure rewards to people who can actually create new wealth." GARY HAMEL

Say it in your own words
The point of re-phrasing the question.

Try always to re-phrase the question in your own words. If you do not understand an idea when it is presented to you, then there is a practical way of finding out whether this is due to the fact that the idea was badly presented or whether it is just a bad and unclear idea packaged in fine words. The trick is to ask the person to describe her idea to you as if you were a child. The point of this Tell-it-to-me-as-if-I-were-a-four-year-old method is that it is hard to hide a fuzzy idea when you describe it to a child.

Many people try to make things so complicated by using corporate bullshit that you do not understand what is wrong, or you end up expending so much energy trying to understand what the problem is that you are too tired to solve it. This phenomenon is increased when ideas come with buzz words like broadband or wireless that people often use carelessly while also finding it difficult to explain what these words mean. This can result in ideas that do not really hold water.

When people explained to Richard Feynman that it was friction that made his leather soles wear out, he replied, *"But what is friction?"* He knew very well what it was, but he wanted people to give him an explanation where they did not just use a word they had learnt to explain a process. He was finally satisfied when he got this as an answer: *"Shoe leather wears out because it rubs against the sidewalk and the little notches and bumps on the sidewalk grab pieces and pull them off."*

As the story *The Emperor's New Clothes* illustrates, children are often good at ignoring smoke screens and detecting the truth. Use this capacity to make your ideas more honest.

ACTIVITY
Does your idea pass the kiddy test? Describe the strong points of your idea as if talking to a child. This sounds like a childish idea, and maybe it is, but nevertheless, it is a very effective way of filtering out those buzz words and bringing out the core of your idea.

Now go one step further and think about what kind of questions a child would ask about how you would develop your idea. This, too, is often a fruitful activity.

"So many of today's management actions such as reengineering and restructuring are based on a deductive kind of thinking. They aim to improve what is. At best, they help a company catch up, but not get on top. They do not lead an organization to develop new hypotheses and create new knowledge. Simply cutting costs and improving business processes no longer is enough." DR. IKUJIRO NONAKA

Rock the boat of certainty

Be sceptical of truths and open to changes.

BACKGROUND

In 1895, the chairman of the British Academy of Science declared that flying machines were a technical impossibility. A couple of years later, the Wright brothers proved that humans could indeed build a craft capable of fulfilling one of humankind's oldest dreams. After this, we were certain that humans would never be able to fly faster than the speed of sound: it was a physical impossibility, we thought. The plane would explode if we were stupid enough to try.

But even this truth had to be modified when the American fighter plane, The Bell x-1, burst the sound barrier in 1947. A passenger plane has been commuting over the Atlantic and breaking the sound barrier for decades now. And up until a couple of years ago, it was thought that space tourism would not be a reality for decades to come. Then the multi-millionaire, Dennis Tito, came along and suddenly 2001 was a good year for a space odyssey if you only had the millions of dollars needed to buy a ticket.

The history of humankind is packed to the seams with truths that later proved not to be true after all, and we cannot understand how people could have been so stupid. Another example: consultants hired by Hewlett-Packard reckoned that there was a market for a maximum of 5,000 calculators. HP ignored the consultants and sold 750,000 calculators in five years.

One of the most quoted misjudgements of all times must be Charles H. Duell's classic utterance from 1899: *"Everything that can be invented has already been invented."* This quotation is so amusing because Duell himself was the head of the American Patents Office and he resigned(!) in 1899 on the grounds that there were no more inventions to be invented.

And sure—it is easy to smile at poor old Duell who missed inventions such as the computer, mobile phone, Internet, spaghetti measure and nuclear weapons—but people who live in greenhouses should not throw stones. We have all been certain of things that have then proved to be untrue. It is even more of a shame that Duell should go down in history for something he did not actually say! An American researcher has spent a lot of time proving that there is no evidence that he actually threatened to resign. In other words, the history is a typical urban myth that has been told so often that we now accept it as the truth. Even though the quotation is not true, the underlying moral is just as strong: never say never. Otherwise, you might end up eating your hat!

ACTIVITY

Write down ten truths about your branch — i.e. things that you are sure will never change — and then see if you can come up with an idea that tears a hole in your truth.

"Heavier-than-air flying machines are impossible."

LORD KELVIN, CHAIRMAN OF THE BRITISH ACADEMY OF SCIENCE, 1895

"Don't worry about people stealing an idea. If it's original, you will have to ram it down their throats."

HOWARD AIKEN

Can it peel pineapples, too?

Plea for a more open climate for ideas.

BACKGROUND

Some people seem to be programmed to find fault with new ideas, to guard the status quo. There is nothing wrong with this as critics and sceptics are also needed. But when there are too many such people, development risks coming to a stop.

Charles Babbage was an inventor and innovator who lived in England in the 1800s. He dabbled in a variety of areas and invented the speedometer, the fundamentals of the cowcatcher and uniform postal rates. Babbage was also the man who designed the forerunner of the modern computer. He visualized a steam-driven machine that could be programmed to carry out different calculations. Unfortunately, he never got to prove that his Difference Engine, and later on his Analytical Engine, actually worked.

He complained about the English person's unwillingness to change: *"Propose to an Englishman any principle, or any instrument, however admirable, and you will observe that the whole effort of the English mind is directed to find a difficulty, a defect, or an impossibility in it. If you speak to him of a machine for peeling a potato, he will pronounce it impossible; if you peel a potato with it before his eyes, he will declare it useless, because it will not slice a pineapple."* In defence of the English, it can be said that they are probably no more critical than most other people, but Babbage's frustration is, unfortunately, shared by many innovators around the world.

ACTIVITY

See if you can manage to listen to 50 ideas without saying anything negative about them. Count the number of positive and negative reactions you get to your next 50 ideas.

"One of the stepping stones to a great world-class operation is to tap into the creative and intellectual power of each and every employee." HARALD A. POLING

Forget what you know and keep on looking!

Most things in life have not been done yet.

We imagine that we know more or less how our branch works, how it will develop and which products and services will be developed in the near future. The truth is, however, that we do not know anything.

Back in 1931, Lincoln Steffens wrote: *"Nothing is done. Everything in the world remains to be done or done over. The greatest painting has yet to be painted, the most moving play yet to be written, the most beautiful poem yet to be recited. Nowhere in the world does there exist the perfect railway, or a good government or a sensible law. Physics, mathematics and, in particular, the most advanced and exact sciences are going through fundamental reviews. Chemistry has become a science; psychology, economics and sociology are waiting for a Darwin, whose work in its turn is awaiting an Einstein. And if the arrogant, naive youths at our university could understand this, then maybe they would not all become specialists in football, drinking sprees and undeserved grades/university degrees. They should not be taught what is already known; they should not be encouraged to learn things that are already known—they are worthless."*

Ingvar Kamprad, the founder of IKEA and one of Europe's most successful businessmen, has the same attitude as Lincoln Steffens. In Kamprad's *Testament of a Furniture Dealer*, there are nine guidelines, the last of which says, *"Most things are yet to be done. Glorious future!"* As one of the nine cornerstones for success, IKEA emphasizes the importance of always trying to find new solutions or ways of doing things, of not doing things in the same old way. Ingvar Kamprad points out the importance of original thinking and innovation. His words have never rung more true than they do today.

ACTIVITY

Sit down and describe what your branch will be like in 1 year, 5 years, 25 years and 100 years. You may argue that it is impossible to guess what will happen in a hundred years' time, but it does not matter if your guess is wrong, for who will be able to correct you? Or, as someone once said, *"In order to discover new continents, you must dare to leave your harbour."*

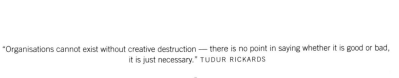

"Organisations cannot exist without creative destruction — there is no point in saying whether it is good or bad, it is just necessary." TUDUR RICKARDS

Ignore what you know

See the strengths and weaknesses of knowledge.

BACKGROUND

At times it seems as if knowledge and creativity were opposites. And this is true, in part, as the more you know about a subject, the more certain you are that you know how it works. You quite literally back yourself into a corner the more you learn about a subject.

In his book *What I know about creativity and innovation*, Bengt-Arne Vedin describes two experiments in creativity that show how earlier experiences stop people from thinking along new lines. The people behind the first experiment invented a new ball game. They then divided the subjects of the experiment into two groups. The first group received instructions about how to hold the raquet and hit the ball before they began to play. The other group was given no instructions at all. They then secretly exchanged the ball for a much heavier one. The group who had not received any special instructions managed the new circumstances much better than those who had learnt how to practise the sport. Their knowledge was an obstacle when the circumstances changed. How many businesses have leaders whose earlier experiences now hinder them from adjusting to the world as it is today?

In the other experiment, two groups were given the task of building a bridge using children's building blocks. When one of the groups entered the room, a bridge of blocks had already been built. This group was influenced by seeing how they could use the blocks, and found far fewer ways of solving their task. They could not think beyond the pre-presented facts.

It is a difficult balancing act as, naturally, knowledge, experience and skills are valuable qualities. It seldom happens that a person without any knowledge in a subject at all comes up with a brilliant new idea. It is just these qualities, however, that can stand in the way of effective development. The trick is to absorb knowledge without getting trapped by it. So, how can we do this?

ACTIVITY

How can we stop our previous knowledge and experience from standing in the way of new ideas? Come up with your own solution to this problem.

"Discovery consists of looking at the same thing as everyone else and thinking something different."
ALBERT VON SZENT-GYÖRYI, PHYSICS NOBEL PRIZE WINNER

Can't see the wood for the trees

Avoid contemplating your navel.

BACKGROUND

Let me tell you a story. A senior executive at Kronägg, Sweden's largest egg producer, receives a phone call during which he and the caller discuss a possible project designed to develop new ideas about how to sell more eggs. The executive decides not to take part in the project, saying, *"All ideas concerning eggs have already been thought of."*

On the one hand, he is right. If there is one person who can claim that all ideas about a product have already been hatched, then who better than a top executive at Kronägg? After all, the egg is probably the world's oldest product (or maybe it is the chicken). On the other hand, most people not working in the egg industry probably realize that there are many ideas about how to sell more eggs that have not been tried out yet. And, of course, this is true: there are plenty of egg-selling ideas that have not yet been thought of. The Kronägg executive, however, is blinded by what he already knows. He thinks that he knows everything there is to know, but everyone still has something to learn. Most of what we think we know just happens to be right at the time.

Let me give you another example. It is the winter of 2001, and I am having a meeting with the Managing Director of one of Sweden's largest Net brokers (stockbrokers trading via the Internet). We sit and discuss the need to think differently and find new solutions to old and new problems. Suddenly, the MD says, *"It is absolutely vital for all businesses to come up with new ideas, except for those of us in banking and finance as we have come up with all the ideas that are possible in the past five years."* Just because there has been such a drastic development in his line of business over the past five years does he seriously believe that there are no more new ideas about how banking and financial services can develop!

ACTIVITY

It is easy to see that there is a lot of room for improvement in other branches, yet so difficult to see that we must improve our own branch in at least as many ways. Try to remember what it was like when you were new at your job. As a new employee, you see things from a new perspective and in a different way, so that in all likelihood, you find things that could be improved. After a year, you suddenly realize that you all too often actively oppose a new employee who comes to the job full of energy and new ideas.

Identify those who prefer to contemplate their navels in your group and have the courage to realize that there are more things that need to change than you think!

"All ideas concerning eggs have already been thought of."

A SENIOR EXECUTIVE AT KRONÄGG

What would happen if...

Use your imagination more.

We do not exercise our imaginations enough. What would happen if you thought 'What would happen if...' a little more often? Well, you would probably come up with more novel ideas and new perspectives about the world you live in. What would happen if companies thought 'What would happen if...' more often? You would probably see more flexible organizations, more open to new ideas. Try it—and see for yourself that imagining 'what if' is easy, useful and surprisingly enjoyable.

What would your company have to do if your customers bought twice as much? What would happen if your customers stopped buying your product tomorrow? What if all bosses turned out to be cartoon characters? What if all the letters in this text make up a secret code you can use to break into Fort Knox? Just imagine!

In a workshop for the marketing department of a well-known European brand name, I asked the participants to try out 'what if' in order to help them see their product with fresh eyes. If your brand were a person, which person would it be? If it were an animal, which animal would it be? and so on. The most memorable moment, however, came when the group was given this task: What would you do if your marketing budget was twice as big? On hearing this question, they looked at each other questioningly until someone piped up, *"We wouldn't do anything differently as we have all the money we need..."* Asking the marketing department of this European company what they would do with twice the budget was like asking Bill Gates what he would do if he had twice the money... However, when I then asked them what they would do if their marketing budget were halved, I was overwhelmed by creative ideas.

ACTIVITY

What would you do if your budget doubled in size? If it were reduced by 50%? Or if you had no budget at all?

"Children enter school as question marks and leave as periods." NEIL POSTMAN

"If you
want to increase
your success
rate, double your
failure rate."

THOMAS J . WATSON, FOUNDER OF IBM

More enquiring minds, please!

Start questioning more.

BACKGROUND

BACKGROUND

"Why do we always do things this way?" children often ask.

We need more enquiring children in business, too, as we would benefit from questioning the status quo more often. When was the last time you questioned something? When was the last time your management questioned its organization? I do not mean that you should overturn decisions as soon as they are made. I just mean that you should question them a little more often.

To question something is often viewed as negative: but it is not. The right amount of questioning is useful as it ensures that we do things in the right way for the right reason. One of the most useful things we can do is question ourselves. When did the finance department of your organization last wonder if too much of their work has been substituted by new technology? When did you last question what you do? When did you last question your boss?

ACTIVITY

Question this activity, this text and this book. Then send your doubts, thoughts and questions to me at: *fredrik.haren@interesting.org*. New ideas that I use in the next version will be rewarded.

"Nothing is more dangerous than an idea, when it is the only idea we have." EMIL CHARTIER

Think like a child

Remember how you thought when you were a child.

BACKGROUND

A character in a cartoon strip says, *"When I was little, my teachers criticized me for drawing outside the lines. Now my boss wonders why I can't think outside the box."*

Young children draw cars with five wheels and engines on the roof. After being corrected many times by adults, they learn that a car should have four wheels and an engine at the front. The VW Beetle, however, has its engine at the back, and there very well may be a good reason to equip a car with five wheels.

Children are not more creative than adults: our creative brain cells do not die off when we grow up. Our experiences in life increase and our brains become better at connecting these experiences with what we already know. The brain wants to create a pattern and connect our observations to our previous knowledge. Preconceived notions, experience, intuition: these are all words for the brain's desire to do what it has always done.

ACTIVITY

Ring your boss and tell her that you are going to work from home for the rest of the day. Then, go to the nearest nursery school and ask if you can sit there and work for a couple of hours. Bring along the problem you are working on and then sit there until you find inspiration and come up with a couple of new solutions. Make sure that you play with the kids while you are there.

"Nothing else in the world ... not all the armies ... is so powerful as an idea whose time has come." VICTOR HUGO

Ideamations

Watch out for ideamations.

BACKGROUND

I have coined the word ideamation, a combination of the words idea and information, which means the first idea that everyone thinks of.

Let me give you an example. If you ask a group of people to think of five different ways of using a brick, then they always come up with at least two of the following suggestions: weapon, bookend, barbecue, pen holder, building material. These five suggestions are not wrong. The problem is that they are ideamations of how to use a brick—i.e. the first ideas that everyone has. There are a myriad ways of using a brick (nail file, fly swatter, coaster, an ingredient in hair dye and so on).

If you ask a group of people to do an advertisement for a company and to use an oil painting in the advert, then a large number of people immediately think of using Da Vinci's Mona Lisa. This painting is also an ideamation of oil paintings used in adverts. No matter what the problem, the first three to five ideas that you have are not ideas but ideamations: solutions that most other people also come up with.

An ideamation is never as valuable as an idea. In order to come up with a unique way of using a brick, you first have to think of lots of ideas. The more unique an idea, the more valuable it is. And the more unique it is, the higher its status as an idea. The problem is that many people think they have had a brilliant idea when, in fact, they have just had an ideamation. It is difficult to distinguish between an idea and an ideamation and the best way of avoiding ideamations is to come up with a lot of ideas.

ACTIVITY

When you come up with a solution to a problem, ask a couple of colleagues to see which solutions they can think of. If one of them has the same idea as you, then your solution is probably an ideamation—and that means that your competitors are likely to have thought of this solution, too. If several people have the same thought, then it diminishes in value. Carry on trying to solve your problem—go a little crazy. It might help.

Ideamation *n. [C]*
the first idea that everyone thinks of.

Think outside the box

Learn to think laterally.

Can you join all nine dots using no more than four strokes and without lifting your pen from the paper?

This is a classic creativity exercise, which is often used to symbolize the importance of finding creative solutions. If you have not seen this puzzle before, then take some time out and try to solve it. Connect all nine dots without using more than four strokes and without lifting your pen. Go to the next section of this book when you think you know the answer.

"Economists around the world are unanimous in believing that innovation is the most important element in the creation of welfare." CHARLES EDKVIST, PROFESSOR AT LINKÖPING UNIVERSITY, SWEDEN

161

Think outside the box *(contd.)*

The solution to the problem of how to connect the dots is usually presented as follows:

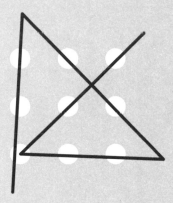

This solution shows very clearly the value of thinking outside the box to solve the problem. 95% of you who thought you 'knew the answer' came up with the same solution as the one you see here. But let's remember what Albert Einstein said: *"I search until I find all of the needles."* There are several ways of solving the puzzle above. As soon as we think we know 'the answer', we continue with our lives.

What would you say if I told you that there were at least three ways of solving the problem in only one stroke? Stop and think again. How can you connect the dots with only one line?

Suddenly, the circumstances have changed—or have they? As soon as we are told to solve the puzzle using no more than four pen strokes, then we have a mental block, and believe that we must do it in four strokes. When we then find out that it is possible to solve the problem with only one stroke, new windows of opportunity suddenly open up. So, what is the solution using only one line?

The first solution is very simple—must a line be straight? Why not draw a curved line through the dots? A line does not have to be straight—and you did not receive instructions to solve the problem using four straight lines. These were only unwritten rules that you set yourself perhaps. But never mind, we can ignore this solution as there are at least three others.

A child's solution — Get hold of a really big, fat felt tip pen and draw a line. The fun of this solution is that you do not even have to go outside the square to solve the puzzle! The solution is as simple as it is ingenious.

Solution two — Put the paper on the ground. Draw a line through the first three dots and then carry on walking around the world. When you get back to your paper, draw a line through the next lot of three dots and walk around the world again. When you get back to the paper, draw a line through the remaining dots. It is a very long line, but it is a line. (Wrap the paper around a globe and do the same thing. Your line is much shorter and you do not have to walk around the world!)

Solution three — This is the most beautiful solution: a Japanese solution based on Origami. By folding the paper in a certain way, you can — with a little practice and patience — line up all nine dots in a long line. Then, all you have to do is draw a line through them. (This is a cocky way of solving the puzzle as well as a good way of winning a bet.)

Solution four — I know a fourth solution, but thought that you should try to find it by yourself...

ACTIVITY

Try to find other ways of solving the puzzle. If you do come up with a new solution, or if you have any suggestions, then send your ideas to me at: *fredrik.haren@interesting.org*

"Many of life's failures are people who did not realize how close they were to success when they gave up."

THOMAS EDISON

What's in a name?

See the strength of naming ideas.

William Shakespeare once wrote:

"What's in a name? that which we call a rose

By any other name would smell as sweet."

But Shakespeare was wrong. Would a rose really smell as sweet if it were called smelly foot rose? Names are powerful tools and they can often help an idea become clearer and sound even better.

There is an island in the West Indies that was once called *Hog Island. Hog Island* was a very beautiful island, but it was difficult to attract tourists to it. Then, one day, a clever person had the bright idea of changing the name of the island and, suddenly, it was inundated by tourists. What was the island's new name? *Paradise Island!*

So, don't use words carelessly. See the power in the meaning of words and use this power to develop your idea.

ACTIVITY

Name your ideas. Don't stop at only one name, but come up with many and do not give up until you have a really good name that not only describes your idea but also enhances it. It is said that the Pacific Ocean was given this name in order not to scare away sailors. What name can you give your idea so that it attracts the right people?

"If someone says that he has learnt to think, most people take it for granted that he has learnt to think logically."
EDWARD DE BONO

Sports creativity

Let the creativity in the world of sports inspire your own.

BACKGROUND

Let me tell you a couple of stories from the world of sports to illustrate how there are always many different ways of solving a task.

The rules for swimming breast stroke stated that swimmers had to move their hands backwards at the same time when under water. There were no rules, however, governing how swimmers should move their hands forwards. In the 1920s, a man discovered that he could swim faster if he moved his hands forward in the air instead of the water—thus inventing the butterfly stroke. The judges quickly realized that although the new swim stroke looked a little strange, it was much faster (up to 15%) than the traditional breast stroke. In order to safeguard the breast stroke, a new swimming style was allowed in which the hands were moved forward above the water: the butterfly. A company that succeeds in finding its equivalent of the butterfly stroke will see its competitors trailing behind as they do the breast stroke.

Sometimes creativity goes to such lengths that sports committees decide to punish original thinking. Do you remember the ingenious Japanese who came up with the idea of climbing(!) up the pole in order to get over the bar (in the pole vault)? This was quickly forbidden. The judges were probably a little shocked as people usually are when someone does something in a completely new way. And when we are shocked, we become defensive. Personally, I think that this is both wrong and cowardly. The purpose of the pole vault is to get over the bar with the aid of a pole—how this is achieved should not matter. (Of course, to forbid throwing the javelin using the same technique as that of hammer throwing (spinning around) is right—for safety reasons, if not for any other reason.)

The example above is one of creative and innovative thinking within well-defined, narrow boundaries (getting over a bar by using a pole). It still shows that you can find completely new—and more effective—ways of solving a problem in spite of limitations. And if we can find better ways of getting over a bar with a pole, then how many better ways are there of doing whatever it is your company does?

Let the world of sport inspire you! How can you use an event from the sporting world to solve your problem?

Or what about the opposite? Use your creativity to develop a sport. For example, can you make curling more interesting to watch?

The ingenious Japanese climbed up the pole...

Metro—a good idea

*Let the idea behind the free newspaper Metro inspire
your own innovative thinking.*

BACKGROUND

Metro is not just a good idea for a newspaper—it also illustrates the fact that
there are unused ideas with enormous potential for business and idea generation in all branches, no matter how conservative and/or old they are.

Let's take a look at the phenomenon of Metro. When Metro (a free morning
newspaper that you can pick up at underground stations in many European
cities) first came out, it was something new. It was not just 'another morning newspaper'. It was a new idea, an innovation. The concept is simple.
Combine the concepts of free newspaper and morning paper and you get
Metro. When you realize that 25% of the costs of publishing a newspaper
is spent on distribution and 25% of the income comes from subscriptions,
then it is easy to see that the figures balance each other. Metro is a simple
idea, but ideas do not need to be complicated to be good or valuable. In
fact, simple ideas are often the most brilliant. None of the old newspaper
publishers or banks dared support the idea of Metro. The newspaper publishers asked, *"What will our owners say?"* and the banks wondered nerv-
ously, *"Has this been done elsewhere before?"*

The old world could not see the value of a new idea. Finally, Metro's three
founders went to the Swedish entrepeneur, Jan Stenbeck. He sat and lis-
tened for nine seconds before saying, *"Here are the one million dollars that
you need."* Stenbeck understood that something of great value is created by
doing that which no one else has done. After two years, Metro had a turno-
ver of approx. 20 million dollars and a four million dollar profit. Within five
years, Metro had succeeded in going from zero readers to being Sweden's
most read morning paper. And in 2001—less than ten years after Monica
Lindstedt and two friends came up with the idea—Metro became the fourth
most popular morning paper in the entire world!

ACTIVITY

Metro is based on the fact that one of the two basic sources of income for a
morning paper has been removed: subscribers. Try to think of a new business idea by taking away the other basic source of income: advertisers.

"Every act of creation is first an act of destruction." PICASSO

179

About TPM & PST

Identify people with TPM and PST.

William Shakespeare wrote: *"Some men never seem to grow old. Always active in thought, always ready to adopt new ideas, they are never chargeable with foggyism. Satisfied, yet ever dissatisfied, settled, yet ever unsettled, they always enjoy the best of what is, are the first to find the best of what will be."*

Shakespeare describes those people who have many more thoughts in a given time period than others. You can almost see how their brains work faster and how new ideas pour forth in a never-ending stream faster than you can snap them up. I call this phenomenon TPM or Thoughts Per Minute. People with a high TPM get a lot of bad, half-baked ideas that are difficult to understand. The last thing you should do is carry out all their ideas as many of them are not well thought out (to put it mildly). However, at the same time, some of their ideas are brilliant. Perhaps we are not more or less creative than the next person—it may just be that certain people come up with many more ideas. And the more ideas we get, the greater the chance of a really, really good idea.

Unfortunately, the world is also full of people who have stopped thinking. I do not mean that their brains have shut down completely—but that they are similar to people who do not take any exercise. We can survive without doing any exercise, but we can do a lot more if we are in good shape. People who've stopped thinking (PST) do what they have always done in life and are sceptical of everyone who seems likely to disturb their comfortable and pleasant existence. Just as a driver who nods off at the wheel can get by as long as the road is straight and nothing changes, so can PST get by as long as everything remains the same. The problem is, of course, that sooner or later the road bends and then the driver is in for an abrupt, often violent, awakening.

ACTIVITY

Identify everyone with a high TPM in your organization and make sure that their skills are put to better use. Also identify those PSTs and try to wake them up from their beauty sleep.

People who've Stopped Thinking (PST) *do what they have always done.*

Brainfire

Let the unconscious do the work.

Brainstorming is a popular way of getting new ideas. Unfortunately, it does not work for the majority. Most people do not get good ideas in groups or at the snap of a finger. Most get brilliant ideas when the brain is not disturbed by trying to think. It is our unconscious that gives us ideas; our conscious seldom comes up with anything new as it is fully occupied bringing forth things we already know and presenting them as new ideas.

When brainstorming, you have a certain amount of time in which to let your conscious come up with ideas. Your unconscious does not have a chance of getting an idea in edgeways.

As a complement to brainstorming, may I suggest Brainfiring? Instead of focusing on getting as many ideas as possible, you work in groups to try and re-phrase the problem that needs solving in a variety of different ways. You then go home and allow the unconscious to work in peace and quiet. You meet again a week later and see what unexpected, unusual ideas have been sown in the calm after the storm.

ACTIVITY

Hold a brainfiring session. Let the group discuss a problem from as many viewpoints as possible for an hour or so. Do not try to solve the problem during this hour, but concentrate on formulating and re-formulating the question. Remember that all problems can be phrased in an endless number of ways and looked at from many different angles. With your head full of problems, go home and let your unconcious get to work. Meet a week or two later and see what ideas have come up.

"It is better to have the philosophy of thinking more than your competitors than spending more than them."
DAVID OGILVY

"Follow the path of the unsafe, independent thinker. Expose your ideas to the dangers of controversy. Speak your mind and fear less the label of 'crackpot' than the stigma of conformity. And on issues that seem important to you, stand up and be counted at any cost."

THOMAS J. WATSON

Blue lights and red cars

It was not always better in the good old days.

BACKGROUND

If you thought that ambulances, fire engines and police cars have blue lights in order to be seen better—then you thought wrong. Emergency vehicles have blue lights in order not to be seen... During the Second World War, the Gestapo began to use blue lights on their cars so as not to disturb the blackout of German cities, which was in force to protect them from the bombers of the Allied Forces. Blue lights are difficult to detect when it is dark. After the war, other police forces continued to use blue lights, although it was totally illogical to do so.

This story about the colour of police lights just goes to show how difficult it can be to introduce a better idea, even though the present one is not effective. The same thing is true of red fire engines. Perhaps you have noticed that ambulances and fire engines in many cities are, in fact, bright yellow? A much more suitable colour for emergency vehicles as bright yellow can be seen more easily in traffic both day and night. Although most of those involved in the fire fighting forces knew that red was not the most suitable colour for the job, it took decades before they dared replace their red vehicles. This might be comforting when you have excellent idea that no one has any time for!

ACTIVITY

Try to identify four routines that are always done in the same way in your branch. Then try to find out what is wrong with them.

"Any business arrangement that is not profitable to the other person will in the end prove unprofitable for you. The bargain that yields mutual satisfaction is the only one that is apt to be repeated." B. C. FORBES

Thinking and re-thinking
Again and again.

When we started interesting.org, we decided that we would actively work towards avoiding the 'stuck-in-a-rut' trap. We do what we call mental somersaults. We even decided that we would sometimes force ourselves to do the opposite of what we would normally do in the most basic things. Take, for example, the ordering of business cards.

It is, without a doubt, common for a company to give its employees business cards. So, we thought, *"What about doing the opposite?"* Our first thought was not to have business cards at all, which may not seem a smart thing to do. However, we followed this line of thinking to see where it would lead. If we did not have business cards, then we would be forced to e-mail our names, addresses and contact numbers to everyone we met—not such a bad idea when you think about it. In fact, it would give us an excuse to get in touch via e-mail and take the contact to the next stage: from meeting to follow-up. We soon realized, however, that our idea of not having business cards also had disadvantages. How practical was it, for example, if the person we met did not have a business card either?

So, we did another mental somersault—that is to say, considered the opposite again. We went from thinking *"Shall we get business cards?"* to *"Let's not get business cards!"* and then re-thought and said, *"Why not get twice as many business cards?"*

And that is what has happened: at interesting.org, we have twice as many business cards. Every time we meet someone, we give them two cards and explain, *"One card is for you and the other is for the most creative person you know so that she or he knows that we exist."* This simple development of the function of the business card has exceeded our expectations. Now people remember us more easily as 'those people who always give out two business cards'.

I have included the example above not because it is a creative idea, but because it shows that even the simplest and most banal tasks that we carry out in our daily life can be improved, changed or done in a completely different way.

Your activity this time is to try to identify a process, product or service that you offer, or to use an idea that, on the surface, appears to be fully developed. See what happens when you think about doing the opposite and then re-think.

Warning! Experience!

Don't trust what you can do too much.

BACKGROUND

I have a friend called Viktor, who has worked as a special needs teacher for many years. After burning out due to his commitment to his students, he decided to quit his job as a teacher. He decided to take a temporary job where he would not need to use his brain. The employment office recommended a job putting up scaffolding.

Viktor started his job on the same day as an autistic boy, who had been given the job because the employment office reckoned that 'this is a job that even you can do'.

Two men with more than ten years' experience already worked for the scaffolding firm. They taught Viktor and the autistic boy how to set up the scaffolding. On the very first day, the autistic boy asked, *"Excuse me, but why not put the two scaffolds together when they are already on the ground, so that we don't have to climb down to fetch the other one?"* The two experienced men looked at each other and were forced to admit that this was a good idea. A couple of hours later, the boy asked again, *"Why not tie the tape to the line so that we always have it with us?"* The two experienced workers looked at each other again, and admitted once more that this was a good idea.

And so it continued. The autistic boy whom the employment office thought could not cope with any other job, was full of ideas about how the work process the two experienced men had used for more than ten years could be improved.

Experience is a costly and valuable treasure, but like all valuable treasures it can also stop people from thinking clearly.

ACTIVITY

Which of your tasks at work do you think are so simple that anyone can do them? How can these tasks be changed or improved?

"Reading, after a certain age, diverts the mind too much from its creative pursuits. Any man who reads too much and uses his own brain too little falls into lazy habits of thinking." ALBERT EINSTEIN

"Fact is,
the first 100 years of our
country's history were about
who could build the biggest,
most efficient farm.

And the second
century focused on the race
to build factories.

Welcome to the third
century, folks.
The third century is
about ideas."

SETH GODIN

Ideas and creativity

An in-depth look at the meaning of the words idea and creativity.

BACKGROUND

Why do we say 'get an idea'? Who do we get the idea from?

We say that we get an idea because our ideas come from God. In the past, people were not creative—only God was. The same thing goes for 'gifted'. The person was not gifted, but had received 'a gift from God'.

Dictionaries are more objective: the Concise Oxford Dictionary describes the word idea like this: *'idea, n. A thought or suggestion as to a possible course of action. A mental impression. A belief.'* Dictionaries are also a good source of more interesting information. The word idea, for example, comes via Latin from the Greek *idea*, which means 'form, pattern'—and is based on *idein* 'to see'.

Creativity is defined as 'relating to or involving the use of imagination or original ideas in order to create something'. The word means making something new, innovative.

Personally, I think the divine explanation reflects what it feels like when you get a good idea: you feel exhilarated, full of energy—and it feels as if you are floating on a cloud. Yes, you can almost feel a god casting a bolt of lightning from the heavens.

ACTIVITY

Buy a dictionary. Next time you are faced with a problem, look up the key word that describes your problem and see what the word means. I promise that this will make it easier for you to generate ideas. And if that does not work, then pray to your God.

"Man, by his essence, is a creative being. Creativity is the basic content of life and the joy of man." IVAN MÁLEK

Can you hire customers?

Find new business.

BACKGROUND

EF (one of the world's largest language learning companies) gave the staffing agency Adecco the task of finding young au pairs to work in the USA. They were to recruit 1,500 young people willing to work as au pairs and study at the same time. In other words, EF paid an agency to find its customers... I like the way EF turned upside down the notion that a staffing agency can only be used to find staff. Suddenly, a whole new world of possiblilities opens up. Will a political party hire people from Manpower to man the voting booths on election day? Can you hire people to vote for your personal election campaign?

All lines of business, no matter how conservative, from politics to shoes will continue to develop as time does not stand still and development cannot be stopped. It is the business with many companies that still believe in development that has the greatest potential for growth.

ACTIVITY

What is the most developed and mature line of business that you can think of? Ask someone who works in this branch what the latest trends are. You will notice that there are many interesting things happening in all businesses at the moment.

"The social consequences of releasing creative abilities are potentially enormous."
J. P. GUILFORD . ONE OF THE WORLD'S LEADING RESEARCHERS IN CREATIVITY

Where do you do your best thinking?

Locate thinking places.

BACKGROUND

You can sometimes hear teachers of creativity talk about the four Bs:

Bars

Bathrooms

Buses

Beds

The four Bs are places where many people feel more creative than usual. Many people have pen and paper on their bedside tables so as to be able to write down all the good ideas they get just before they nod off. There are numerous stories about brilliant business ideas that were thought of in bars and restaurants, and quickly noted down on paper napkins before the divine creative force disappeared. I would also like to add a fifth B: boring meetings, and say that these are only good for generating ideas in subjects that have nothing to do with the boring meeting in question.

It is said that Beethoven stimulated his brain by pouring ice-cold water on his head, and Albert Einstein got his best ideas when shaving. Yes—most people have one or more places where they can think better than usual. I myself think best when travelling, whether by bus, car or train. As long as I am not driving, my brain embarks on its own fascinating journeys.

ACTIVITY

Where do you think best? Identify these places and then make sure that you work there more often. Do you think best in the shower perhaps? Then shower more during working hours!

At more than a hundred lectures I have asked the audience, *"Where do you get your best ideas?"* As well as the four Bs, I often get answers like this: *"When I run." "When I play with my kids." "When I'm exercising."* Seldom has anyone answered, *"When I'm at work."*

There is a Dilbert cartoon strip where Dilbert is filling out his time report:
Five hours at a long, unproductive meeting = work. Half an hour in the
shower thinking of improvements to my design = leisure. Scott Adams
has a way of hitting the nail on the head.

Bb*Bb*

Knowing that you do not know anything

You and I are wrong more often than we think.

BACKGROUND

"There is only one thing about which I am certain, and that is that there is very little of which one can be certain," said Somerset Maugham.

Creative people are often quick to confess that they do not know everything, and even that we humans know only a fraction of everything that there is to know.

Thomas Edison, for example, said, *"We don't know a millionth of one percent about anything."* And Bertrand Russel wrote, *"The trouble with the world is that the stupid are cocksure and the intelligent are full of doubt."* Or why not listen to the wise words of Amelia Adamo, Swedish newspaper entrepreneur. *"The day you think you know everything, then you are a danger to the company."*

Why is it so difficult to confess that we do not have all the answers? Why so hard to say that we feel uncertain or that we do not know what is going to happen? History is littered with people who were absolutely sure — but completely wrong — about things. Maybe it is just normal for people to believe that they are in full control. Remember that it is not the same thing as you being in full control!

Lao-Tzu once said: *"To know yet to think that one does not know is best; Not to know yet to think that one knows will lead to difficulty."* Throw that into the face of the next person who thinks that he (it is most often a he) has all the answers.

ACTIVITY

Write down three things you were completely sure of, but which you have now realized you were wrong about. Yes, I know it is hard to admit you are wrong, but believe me, it is irritatingly good for you!

"We must... become adept at learning. We must become able not only to transform our institutions, in response to changing situations and requirements; we must invent and develop institutions [and societies] that are 'learning systems', that is to say, systems capable of bringing about their own continuing transformation." DONALD A. SCHON, INNOVATION THEORIST

Find new inspiration

Look for new sources of inspiration.

BACKGROUND

It is claimed that André Gide tried to read at least one book a month about a subject that did not interest him. Have you ever tried this?

In order to get new ideas, you must also get new influences. Yet, most company executives read The Financial Times, The Economist, Fortune or the Wall Street Journal. And then they read papers relating to their own lines of business, which all company executives read too. I would like to see all managers reading ten different papers about businesses far removed from their own. What can a manager, say, learn from reading Parenting Today or Dolphin Trainer? Masses! I myself do not subscribe to any newspapers, but I do have an office opposite a newsagency where I get a 10% reduction on everything they have in stock. I go there every week and buy at least one paper I have never read before.

To read an article from International Meats, for example, about how the terrorist attacks of September 11th affected the meat business is more rewarding than it sounds. I definitely learned something from reading that article!

John Taylor of GM's APEX department, which manufactures extreme concept cars, once explained why his department stopped going to car exhibitions. His main argument was that everyone in the automobile business goes to the same exhibitions and that is why they all come up with the same ideas. Instead, John Taylor and his team began to attend computer game and toy exhibitions, and fashion shows. If you think about it, it is easy to see that a car designer can find as much inspiration from a toy exhibition as a car exhibition. Probably more. And they probably had a better time, too.

ACTIVITY

Go into your newsagent's and buy three papers that you did not even know exist. Then sit down with a cup of hot chocolate to read them and be inspired.

"Our present problems are not primarily political or economic but are rooted in the inadequate use of our humanity, or, rather, in our persistence in using those capacities in ourselves that are no longer appropriate to the present times."
JEAN HOUSTON, PROFESSOR OF RELIGION AND PHILOSOPHY

223

Are you really going to throw that out?!

See the value of worthless things.

BACKGROUND

I read somewhere in an old American advertising book that crushed pineapple was 'invented' long after pineapple rings. When pineapple rings were first sold, the bits that were not whole or big enough were just thrown away. After a while, someone came up with the idea of crushing these scraps of pineapple and selling them as crushed pineapple. Something that was once scraps was turned into a huge success.

Or what about the company that rents out storms during the summer by using the snow machines of ski resorts that are shut? The tent manufacturer Hilleberg has sometimes used this service to see if their tents can be put up in the middle of a raging storm. The world is full of worthless things of value.

ACTIVITY

Sit down with a colleague and talk about the waste products your company produces. Why are they deemed worthless? Or consider this: what do you see as a cost or expense and how could you turn this into a source of income?

"Necessity is the mother of invention." LUCIUS APULEIUS

Crime and punishment

Can we learn something from the criminal?

BACKGROUND

Human creativity is perhaps greatest in the criminal. Perhaps we can even learn something about the power of thinking differently from criminals. Take, for example, the story of a prison, Korydallos, in Athens as described in a newspaper article. *"Hardened prison guards have seen almost everything under the sun here. A female visitor was arrested for trying to take a bowl of french fries to one of the prisoners—she had filled the potato slices with heroin. (...) The guards had good reason to be watchful. Friends and relatives are using increasingly strange ways of smuggling drugs into the prison. A few months ago, a woman smuggled in heroin to her grandchild in a bowl of spaghetti."*

Or what about this as an example of the creative development of services? A financial paper reported the story of how the time share business 'developed' new services in the form of a 'legal aid company'. The legal aid company phoned up people cheated in time share deals to offer to help them get their money back. All the victims had to do was to pay 300 dollars to cover the costs... And the poor, trusting foreigners had been hoodwinked once again.

ACTIVITY

There are new opportunities in all businesses, even in time shares, for those who think creatively. Which opportunities exist in your line of business?

About unwritten laws
And the punishment for breaking them.

BACKGROUND

Whenever we face a problem, there are always certain boundaries that we have to stick to. These can be laws and regulations, laws of nature and/ or mental limitations. Unfortunately, most people are so anxious not to break the rules that they even set up their own in order to be on the safe side. After twelve years at school, we are so frightened of being accused of 'cheating' that we would rather enforce a couple of our own rules and regulations instead of trying to break the ones that already exist. The more boundaries and limitations we set up, the less creative space we have in which to come up with new ideas.

Let me tell you a story about breaking unwritten rules so that you will never forget that creativity is all about breaking the mould and not creating it.

The story takes place in a large casino in Las Vegas. A croupier is standing at one of the tables, spinning a roulette wheel. After a lot of spinning, the ball comes to rest on number 7. A man standing next to the table yells in disappointment, *"No!"* He then gives the croupier ten dollars. As the man has not placed any chips, the surprised croupier asks him why he gave him the ten dollars. The man replies, *"I made a mental bet of ten dollars on number 19, and I lost."* The croupier sighs resignedly and takes the money.

The same procedure is repeated several times; the man gives the croupier ten dollars every time he places a mental bet and loses. Suddenly, the ball lands on number 17 and the man shouts with joy, *"Yippee! I bet 10,000 dollars in my mind that the ball would land on number 17."* The croupier, of course, thinks that the man is kidding, but he is deadly serious and sues(!) the casino. His argument in court is that if the casino accepts mental bets when someone loses, then they ought to accept them when they win...

The unlikely happens: the judge rules in the man's favour, but adds an important statement. *"A casino that accepts mental bets must also pay out mental winnings. However, it is all right for a casino to pay mental winnings with mental cheques..."*

The moral of the story is this: it is seldom dangerous to break an unwritten rule.

Which unwritten rules are there in your business that no one dares break, but which would probably have a positive effect if someone did break them?

"The only person who likes change is a wet baby."

ROY Z-M BLIZER

Be an upstart

Question the truths of your line of business.

Only a few years ago were budget airlines something the big, established airlines sneered at. After all, they were not 'real' airline companies and would never be a threat to the lucrative business airlines. Well-established companies often find it difficult to see new business opportunities as they have their hands full earning money doing what they have always done. Development is left to the young, new upstarts. And in the case of the budget airlines, it was the upstart who got the longest straw.

Today, Ryanair is one of the few profitable airline companies in Europe. Development has not stopped at the low price airfare, however. Tomorrow's winner is written in the stars — or, at least, high up among the clouds. While waiting for a new competitor to develop the airline business, Ryanair launched a new concept: free flights.

Ryanair's CEO, Michael O'Leary, told reporters how the company plans to introduce free flights and make money on in-flight gaming machines instead. *"We plan to be a kind of airborne Las Vegas,"* he said. This is definitely a creative use of the 'swings and roundabouts' strategy.

ACTIVITY

How could you package a product in your line of business so that it appears to be free? When did the last upstart in your business appear and what did they see that no one else did? Which area could a potential upstart concentrate on to really make some waves in the business?

What's in an icon?

About the 'we-have-always-done-it-like-this' illness.

BACKGROUND

When Apple released their ground-breaking computer, iMac, Steve Jobs and co. chose to deliver it without a floppy disk drive. Apple's argument was that using diskettes was a stone age technology in the Internet age. However, in Microsoft's new Office software package for Apple's operating system OS X, the 'Save' symbol is still a diskette...

There is a story about a boot factory in Norway that brought in a consultant to make the organization more effective. The consultant came across a woman whose job was to jot down in a little book how many pairs of boots were made during each shift. When the book was full, she filed it with hundreds of other books. When the consultant asked what the purpose was of writing down the exact number of boots manufactured per shift, the woman replied that she did not really know why, but that things had always been done this way.

After a little detective work, it was discovered that, during the Second World War, the Germans had ordered the factory to keep an inventory of the number of boots so that the company could not make boots for the resistance in secret. The reason for this routine became redundant more than forty years ago... Just because you have always done things in a special way does not mean that you should continue to do so.

ACTIVITY

Will the 'Save' symbol still be a picture of a diskette in ten years' time, when many computer users will not know what a diskette is? Which symbol for saving data on a computer would be more suitable?

"Follow the path of the unsafe, independent thinker. Expose your ideas to the dangers of controversy. Speak your mind and fear less the label of 'crackpot' than the stigma of conformity. And on issues that seem important to you, stand up and be counted at any cost." THOMAS J. WATSON

Everything begins now

A society of information or innovation?

BACKGROUND

"Eleven billion people have lived since creation, and six billion are still alive today. Why should we spend so much time on what the five billion who are dead did? I prefer to look forwards. That is why I buy modern furniture, contemporary art and build completely new houses." The Swedish entrepreneur, Bertil Hult, said this in a newspaper interview on 13th April, 2002.

Bertil Hult has a point (even if most calculations indicate that 1/20 of all those born are alive today, and not half). If we were to count everyone who has had an education and learnt to read and write, then an overwhelming majority are alive today.

As if that thought were not dizzying enough, what about the following? Of all the information that has ever been written down up to the year 2000, 12%(!) was written in 1999. Or what about this? Between 1970 and 1985, the number of documents in Sweden doubled. That is, it took 15 years. Now, the number of documents double every three months.

The statistics go on… But the question is if we really understand what the change indicated by the figures above is going to mean.

ACTIVITY

We stand on the brink of an information and innovation explosion the like of which we have never seen before. Are you ready?

An overwhelming majority of all researchers who have lived are active today. How will this influence the development of innovation in the next fifty years? What will they think of that has not yet been imagined?

"It is useless to send armies against ideas." GEORGE BRANDES

Crealogical and logical

Different types of thinking.

BACKGROUND

It is said that the left half of the brain is the brain's logical part. It is there that you find language and mathematics, order and structure. To think logically can be both effective and useful, but we in the West are, unfortunately, a little too good at thinking logically.

I suggest that, instead, you adopt a more 'crealogical' way of thinking. Crealogical thinking is the opposite of logical thinking. A logical person has a well-organized desk, while a crealogical person has everything lying in big piles on the desk, but they still know where to find everything important...

Crealogical can best be described as creative chaos or illogical logic. Other examples of crealogical thinking are birds flying together in flocks, ants building their ant hills or the way snow falls. They are all examples of things that work as they should without any visible, logical control.

ACTIVITY

Of course, crealogical thinking is just something I have invented! But you must agree that we need a counterbalance to logical thinking. Think of a current problem and write down a logical solution to it. Then try to find a crealogical solution to the problem—i.e. come up with an answer that, on the surface, seems chaotic.

"Men who accomplish great things in the industrial world are the ones who have faith in the money producing power of ideas." CHARLES FILLMORE

That's impossible!

Be sceptical of impossibilites.

BACKGROUND

In my workshops on creativity, I usually ask the public to think of something that is impossible. Every third suggestion is, *"It is impossible for man to fly."* Another third say, *"Teleporting is impossible."*

An article at www.idg.se describes how researchers have already succeeded in carrying out a kind of teleporting: *"In 1997, a team of researchers at Innsbruck University proved that the method works when they managed to teleport the properties of a light particle about a metre. The transportation was immediate. The researchers had just carried out the world's first teletransportation."*

Remember that creativity flourishes when you never say never. Personally, I am quite convinced that a person will fly before I die. (All you have to do is clone a person with a swan...)

ACTIVITY

Think of something that is impossible. Many people find this very difficult and, surprisingly often, I hear suggestions that the majority of my audience is certain will be possible in the future. We are just too unaccustomed to coming up with really wild ideas.

"A new and valid idea is worth more than a regiment and fewer men can furnish the former than command the latter."
OLIVER WENDELL HOLMES, JR.

Columbus

1492's innovative thinker.

When Christopher Columbus presented his idea of sailing westwards in order to reach India to King Ferdinand of Spain, the king sighed and said, *"Procura cura para to locura."* Or, as we say in English, *"Go get your head examined!"* Most people thought that the visionary Italian was crazy. Columbus' own calculations as to how far away India really was may have been wrong—but his courage just goes to show that it can be worthwile sailing in the wrong direction.

On his return from his voyage, Columbus was at a dinner party where several dinner guests began to mock him. *"So, you've discovered some new, distant lands, have you? So what? Anyone can sail across the ocean and come across a deserted island like you did. What's the big deal?"*

Columbus did not answer. Instead, he got up and fetched an egg. He then turned to the men and asked, *"Can any of you stand this egg up on its end?"* All of the men tried, but without any success. They finally agreed that it was impossible. Columbus took the egg and banged it on the table so that the bottom of the hard-boiled egg cracked. He then stood the egg on the table. *"Gentlemen,"* he said. *"Any one of you can now get the egg to stand on its end. It's the easiest thing in the world—once you've been shown how to do it!"*

The story of Columbus and the egg illustrates two things: that good ideas are often very simple, and that good ideas are often perceived to be obvious after they have been thought of. It is difficult for us to confess that we, ourselves, did not come up with a good idea when we hear of one.

Do you remember the example earlier on in this book: that if Nokia made cars, would we be able to choose horn melodies? Just as it is obvious today that we should be able to choose ring signals for our mobile phones, so was it equally obvious not so long ago that a phone should go 'Ring! Ring!' when it rang. Things that are unthinkable today will be obvious tomorrow.

Jot down three ideas that you thought were simple once you had heard them. Then describe what it is that makes these ideas so simple—and brilliant.

"*Can any of you stand this egg up on its end?*"

Discover the unique

Let us tempt you with three brain teasers!

Here are three graphic puzzles to pit your wits against. Each puzzle consists of five shapes. One of them is unique and differs from the others. Which one? And above all—why?

The connection is not always obvious. Try looking at the puzzles from many different angles!

FACE LIFT

A   B   C   D   E

MODERN GALLERY

A   B   C   D   E

CHEMISTRY

A   B   C   D   E

You will find the answers on page 281.

"It wasn't my idea. But I don't give a damn."

DESTINY PLAYBACK

Newledge

You can't do something just because you can.

BACKGROUND

A hundred years ago, 700(!) students graduated from the equivalent of senior high or upper secondary school in Sweden. In 2001, there were between 90,000 and 100,000 upper secondary school graduates. As late as 1960, only 30,000 Swedes attended university compared to today's figures of 300,000 (of which 30,000 are postgraduates). We are only talking about Sweden here. If we compare how many people in the entire world have a university education today with those fifty years ago — then the figures are amazing! And it is almost frightening to think what the figures will be like in fifty years' time.

The recent knowledge explosion has led to a dramatic increase in new knowledge. And the more new knowledge we learn about, then the more old knowledge is just that: old. Certain university courses in the USA have stopped using course books as they become outdated too quickly. The students read relevant magazines and other publications with faster printing times.

Everyone says that we have to be better at taking in knowledge, but surely it is new knowledge — newledge — we should be trying to acquire? It is not hard to learn something. But to re-learn it is trickier.

The world is full of professionals — from blacksmiths to newspaper graphic designers — who are no longer needed because they were too good at doing what they already could, but too bad at learning something new.

ACTIVITY

When did you last learn something new? In other words, when did you last go on a course in a subject you already 'knew' in order to see if you could learn the same thing in a new way?

"There is nothing in the world more powerful than an idea. No weapon can destroy it; no power can conquer it except the power of another idea." JAMES ROY SMITH

YES and NO!

About positive conflicts.

BACKGROUND

Once upon a time, kings always had a jester. The jester's job was to question truths and ask questions that no one else dared to ask. The jester was the king's protection against the yes-men. Why did the jester's role disappear? Not because yes-men do not exist anymore! On the contrary, the need for opposition is greater than ever, as creativity does not flourish when everyone thinks alike. When asked what creates a good car, Toyota's Development Manager replied, *"A lot of conflicts."* A senior CIA boss was heard to exclaim on the Discovery channel, *"We need sceptics! If we don't get criticism, then we'll hire a sceptic!"*

Perhaps it is wrong to encourage more conflicts, but surely it is just as wrong to encourage even fewer? Unfortunately, too many people have learned never to criticize an idea. This is totally wrong. Good ideas tolerate criticism and bad ideas do not improve if no one points out their weaknesses. We all know that homogenous groups where everyone shares the same knowledge, the same background and the same references are those who are less likely to succeed when circumstances change. Even so, far too many groups, from small project teams to big company management groups, tend to be homogenous. And, of course, it is comfortable when everyone thinks the same, isn't it?

ACTIVITY

Go looking for negative comments. Next time you have a good idea, go and look for someone who does not like it. Let that person criticize it in detail and write everything down. Then go home and look through the list of criticism and try to see the idea's weak points. This activity is tough—but also worthwhile.

"It is useless to close the gates against ideas; they overlap them." KLEMENS VON METTERNICH

Airplanes and computers

It never turns out as you imagine.

When Apple produced their first versions of the laptop, they built their entire strategy on the fact that laptops would only be used by business executives on airplanes. The company spent a lot of time, amongst other things, on making sure that the computers would work with the aircraft's electronics. After the laptops were launched, Apple managers held a crisis (!) meeting to discuss the fact that the laptops were used everywhere except on airplanes.

The future seldoms turns out as we imagine it will. Question all visions of the future and assume that everyone is wrong rather than right. The chances are greater this way that you are right...

Next time someone describes a vision of the future to you, question it. Ask the person for alternative futures. You will notice that most people have only one view of what the future will be like. If you take this book out again in ten years, then you will find that all your friends were wrong.

"Ideas are the factors that lift civilization. They create revolutions.
There is more dynamite in an idea than in many bombs." BISHOP VINCENT

Discover the unique
(solutions)

Here are the solutions (and reasons why) to the graphic puzzles from page 266. Please note that our answers are not necessarily the ones that are right for you. It is more important to really think about the puzzles and then motivate your answers!

FACE LIFT

They all follow the laws of physics, except for (a).

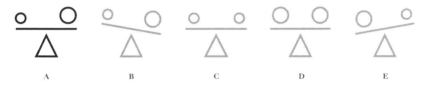

A   B   C   D   E

MODERN GALLERY

(c) is the only one in which the three rectangles overlap each other.

A   B   C   D   E

CHEMISTRY

All the bubbles have the same size sequence from bottom to top, except (e).

A   B   C   D   E

These graphic enigmas are designed by André Wognum. Try mobile the phone game at www.epicbrain.com!

Do not give up

Inspiration not to give up.

"I've got a sort of idea," said Pooh at last, *"but I don't suppose it's a very good one." "Probably not,"* said Eeyore.

I would like to conclude this book by urging you to dare to think differently. People who question the status quo, who continue to look for new ideas and who refuse to believe that everything is fine as it is, often have a hard time. It is all too easy to run down someone else's ideas, and it is not always easy to stand up for your own ideas—especially if these ideas are, in some way, controversial, different or rebellious.

But do not give up. The joy you get from coming up with a new idea and then seeing it turned into reality is worth the trouble. If you need encouragement or inspiration in generating ideas, then read the text to Apple's 'Think Different' advertising film:

> *Here's to the crazy ones,*
>
> *the misfits, the rebels, the troublemakers.*
>
> *The round pegs in the square holes.*
>
> *The ones who see things differently.*
>
> *They are not fond of rules and they have no respect for the status quo.*
>
> *You can quote them, disagree with them, glorify or vilify them.*
>
> *But the only thing you can't do—is ignore them.*
>
> *Because they change things.*
>
> *They push the human race forward.*
>
> *And while some may see them as the crazy ones, we see genius.*
>
> *Because the people who are crazy enough to think they can change the world—are the ones who do.*
>
> *Think Different.*

ACTIVITY

You are probably fed up with doing activities, so let's finish the book here instead!

"Great ideas need landing gear as well as wings." C. D. JACKSON

283

Conclusion

Thank you for taking the time to read this book. I hope that it has acted as a tool to help you generate new ideas. Do not forget to go back and read your old notes and ideas now and then. Sometimes ideas improve if left to mature a little.

If you have a favourite story about creativity or have recently heard of a company that has done the opposite—then share your stories with me! Everyone who sends in anecdotes that I have not heard before and that I include in The Idea Book 2 will receive a free copy of the new book and 100 dollars as thanks.

You can contact me at *fredrik.haren@interesting.org* or on my mobile: *+46 705 86 18 18.*

fredrik.haren@interesting.org

Inspiration

Here is a list of a few of the books and people who inspired me while writing this book.

BOOKS THAT HAVE INSPIRED ME

The Art of Innovation, Tom Kelley

Creativity & Beyond, Robert Paul Weiner, 2000

Den kreativa människan, SVD Pocket, 1983

Du är kreativ, Michael LeBoeuf, Liber, 1980

Funky Business, Jonas Ridderstrale, Kjell Nordstrom, Financial Times Prentice Hall, 2000

Kodboken, Simon Singh, Norstedts förlag 1999

Pippi in the South Seas, Astrid Lindgren, Rabén & Sjögren, 1948

Flow, Michály Csíkszentmihályi, NOK, 1996

Salvatore Grimaldi, Salvatore Grimaldi, Ekelids Förlag 2000

Uppfinnaren, Alf Mork, Atlantis, 1981

100 råd om innovation, Bengt-Arne Vedin, Ljusåret, 1998

Skapandets psykologi, Frak Barron, Alma, 1971

Fantasins Grammatik, Gianni Rodari, Korpen, 1973

A Whack on the side of the head, Roer von Oech, Warner Books, 1998

Kreativitet – en outnyttjad resurs, Dag Romell, Liber Läromdelel, 1974

Edison: A life of Invention, Paul Israel, John Wiley & Sons, 1998

Brain boosters for business advantage, Arthur B VanGundy. Joeesey-Bass/Pfeiffer, 1995

Notebooks of the mind, Vera John-Steiner, Oxford University Press, 1997

Influence, Science & Practice, Robert B Cialdini, Harper Collins, 1993

Tankekraft, Bodil Jönsson, Brombergs, 2001

Deals of lightning, Michael A Hiltzik, Harper Business, 2000

75 Cage-Rattling Questions to change the way you work, Dick Whitney Melissa Giovangnoli, McGraw Hill, 1997

The Mechanism of mind, Edward de Bono, Penguin Books, 1969

Selling the invisible, Harry Beckwith, Warner Books, 1997

Fursten, Niccoló Machiavelli, NoK, 1513

Yates' Guide to successful inventing, Raymond Yates, Funk & Wagnalls, 1967

Citat för alla tillfällen, Brombergs, 2001

The art of creation, Arthur Koestler, Picador, 1969

Unleashing the idea virus, Seth Godin, Do you Zoom?, 2000

Svar:, Anna Thurfjell, Carlssons, 2000

Att bryta vanans makt, Vernet Denvall, Studentlitteratur, 2000

The book of truly stupid business quotes, Jeff Parietti, HarperPerennial, 1997

Upptäckter som förändrade världen, David Elito Brody & Arnold Brody, MånPocket, 1997

Nätokraterna, Alexander Bard & Jan Söderqvist, K-world, 2000

The inmates are running the asylum, Alan Cooper, Sams, 1999

Cracking Creativity, Michael Michalko, Ten speed Press, 1998

Uncommon Genius, Denise Shekerjian, Penguin, 1990

Collaborative Creativity, Jack Ricchiuto, Oakhill Press, 1997

Träffad av en snilleblixt, Roger von Oech, Odulate Förlag, 1987

Creative thinking and brainstorming, J Geoffrey Rawlinson, Management Skills Library, 1981

Verklig kreativitet, Edward de Bono, Brainbooks, 1992

Creativity, George Gamez, Peak Publications, 1996

Idéer, så får du dem så utvecklar du dem, Jack Foster, Richters, 1999

Handbook of creativity, Robert J Sternberg, Cambridge, 1999

Ett svenskt geni, David Lagercratz, DN förlag, 2000

Speaker's sourcebook 2, Glenn Van Ekeren, Prentice Hall, 1994

Din upphovsrätt och andras, Kerstin Ahlberg, Tiden, 1995

Christofer Columbus, var han riktigt klok, Herman Lindqvist, Fischer & co, 1992

2000 percent solution, Donald Mitchell mfl, Amacom, 1999

Patafysisk Antologi, Claes Hylinger, Bo Cavefors Förlag, 1973

Copy, Hal Stebbins, Spektra, 1974

Människor, miljöer och kreativitet Nobelpriset 100 år, Red, Ulf Larsson, Atlantis, 2001

Den vite mannen, Papalagi, Korpen, 1920

The art of looking sideways, Alan Fletcher, Phaidon, 2001

Alice i Underlandet, Lewis Caroll, nyöversättning, Bokorama, 1982

Awaken your birdbrain, Bill Costello

Guldägg och beska droppar, Sören Blanking, Fischer & Co, 1996

A designer's art, Paul Rand, Yale University Press, 1985

Where the Suckers Moon: The Life and Death of an Advertising Campaign, Randall Rothenberg, 1995

Think out of the box, Mike Vance & Diane Deacon, Career Press, 1995

Don't Panic, Troed Troedson & Lotta Alsén, Troedson Konsult, 2002

The Creative Problem Solver's Toolbox, Richard Fobes, Solutions Through Innovation, 1993

Rules for revolutionaries, Guy Kawasaki, Harper Business, 1999

Creative Thinking, Mike Vance, audio book

Teo Härén

Marie Thorsbrink

Albert

Berit Härén

Hasse Härén

Torbjörn Härén

André Wognum

Maria Ehn-Notrica

Mårten Norman

Andreas Pardeike

Jocke Berggren

Fredrik Ahlman

Erik Reimhult

Bengt-Arne Vedin

Bengt Renander

Yngve Bergqvist

Leif Pagrotsky

Marie Hallander Larsson

Mats Ohlsson

Maria Blom

Fabian Månson

Kerstin Karlsson

Therese Foleby

Alexander Bard

Gustav Bard

Anders Carlberg

Amelia Adamo

Soki Choi

Philip Cohen

Monica Lindstedt

Bengt Möller

Marita Bohlin

Tommy Karman

Thomas Magnusson

Lars Fallberg

Petra Pardeike

Lars Larsson

Christer Skoglund

Jack Hansen

Jan Segerfeldt

Anette Gustafsson

Jan Linnaeus

Ann Westfelt

+ everyone who helped with the proofreading of this book in one way or another!

All the members of interesting.org and your wonderful ideas!

And finally, Anna Breitholtz—for inspiring me more than I thought was possible and more than you can understand.

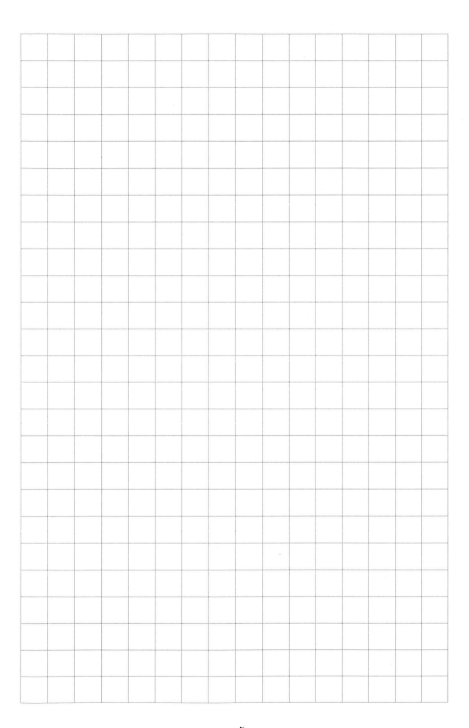

About the interesting organisation (interesting.org)

The Interesting Organization is Sweden's leading creativity company and is most active in Northern Europe and Asia. Our vision is to inspire others and each other to get more ideas and make them a reality.

The Interesting Organization helps people and organizations become more innovative and creative. And as no two people or companies are alike, we do this in many different ways. From creative coaching of managerial groups to individual coaching of company presidents; from workshops about how to develop creativity and generate ideas to helping companies develop long-term creativity strategies.

We are also well known for our successful keynote speeches, lectures and workshops about creativity, innovation and idea generation as well as for our best-selling series of Idea Books and other creativity tools.

Contact us at www.interesting.org and let us know what challenges you are facing. We will let you know how we can help you and, of course, provide relevant references from among our thousands of satisfied customers.

About The Idea Book

The Idea Book has sold more than 200,000 copies around the world and has been published in eleven languages: English, Swedish, Norwegian, Lithuanian, Japanese, Thai, Tagalog, Chinese, Sinhalese, Tamil and Icelandic. The book was so popular in Iceland that 3,000 copies were sold in a month – meaning that it only took 30 days for 1% of the population to come in contact with the book!

The Idea Book was recently included in the American book "The 100 Best Business Books of all Time" by Jack Covert and Todd Sattersten.

Book a lecture or workshop

Invite your co-workers or customers to an inspiring seminar on business creativity. To a lecture about the importance and value of new ideas. Or to an uplifting talk that encourages creativity and innovative thinking.

Fredrik's lectures help the audience understand how valuable it is to think in new ways – and how difficult this is to achieve.

Fredrik was voted Speaker of the Year in Sweden, so if someone can give a good speech, he can. He lectures around the world and has given speeches in more than 5o countries ranging from China and Japan to the USA and Canada.

Satisfied customers include The Swedish Parliament, Hewlett Packard, China Mobile, Ogilvy and American Express and many, many more.

About the author

Fredrik is a renowned speaker and one of Sweden's most popular lecturers. He has held more than 1,500 speeches, seminars and workshops for well over 100,000 people in 50 different countries around the world.

Co-author

The co-author of this book is Teo Härén (teo.haren@interesting.org), who has also done much of the research. He is the CEO and founder of interesting.org and during the past few years, he has read, sorted, assessed and rated more than 30,000 business development ideas. If there is someone who can tell a good idea from a bad one—then it is Teo.

Graphic design

The graphic designer of this book is André Wognum—a creator whose breadth and depth is hard to come by. André has designed everything from virtual worlds to company trademarks (www.wognum.se).

Translator

The translator of this book is Fiona Miller, a love immigrant from Britain, who came to Sweden in search of a writing job back in 1996 and who has been stranded there due to the snow (and a husband) ever since.

Fiona is the author of more than ten educational books as well as co-author of a TV series designed to teach English to China. These days, she dabbles in anything interesting and creative—such as writing scripts for interactive media and translating books like this one!

Tell a friend

Ideas are there to be passed on! And good ideas should be rewarded. Do you know someone who would buy large quantities of The Idea Book? Then do this:

1. Send an e-mail to the person in question and recommend this book. (Tell them about: *www.theideabook.org* too!)

2. Send a copy of your mail to: *fredrik.haren@interesting.org.*

3. If your contact orders more than ten books, then you get a commission.

For your company

This book is based on the belief that all organizations must become much better at encouraging more creative thinking. For information and prices regarding books for some/all of your employees, please send an e-mail to: *info@interesting.org.*

www.theideabook.org

The book's own web site.